PICTORIAL HISTORY of NEWMILNS

James Mair

COVER:
Oil Painting of old Newmilns
by Hugh Rankin

© James Mair, 1988

First Published in 1988
by Alloway Publishing Ltd.,
Darvel, Ayrshire.

Printed in Scotland
by Walker & Connell Ltd.,
Hastings Square,
Darvel, Ayrshire.

ISBN 0-907526-34-9

ALL RIGHTS RESERVED
No part of this publication may be reproduced, stored in a retrieval system, or transmitted in any form or by any means without the prior permission in writing of the publisher, nor be otherwise circulated in any form of binding or cover other than that in which it is published and without a similar condition including this condition being imposed on the subsequent purchaser.

PICTORIAL HISTORY of NEWMILNS

James Mair

INTRODUCTION

"A Pictorial History of the Irvine Valley" was originally conceived as a single volume work. However it soon became evident, with the amount of material available, that it would be necessary to publish in three parts one each for Newmilns, Galston and Darvel and their adjoining districts, thus retaining the individual character of each place, but still acknowledging the wider sense of community which exists resulting from close proximity of the three towns in the upland Irvine Valley.

In times past people from each town felt aggrieved if mistaken for a resident of another, but each was happy to be recognised by outsiders as a person from "up the Valley". The fierce rivalry of former years has mellowed, now that the independence of the three small burghs has been wrested from them, but affection for the district as a whole has survived.

The three volumes of photographs are intended to record the Valley towns and their inhabitants when small was still beautiful or, as the Scots proverb has it — *Guid gear gangs in sma buik*. What is often now described as parochialism was once seen as an intense pride of place, and the feeling that your own town lay at the centre of the universe. This sometimes verged on the ludicrous as, on a day in 1910 an old citizen enquired into the purpose of the largest procession ever arranged in the town, as it moved towards the parish kirk. When he was told it was for the funeral of King Edward, his undaunted reply was "Oh, I didna ken he was tae be buried in Newmulls."

Stories with the same flavour are legion, but old photographs are elusive and perishable. Selections are limited to what the early camera enthusiasts considered worthy subjects. Country views and street scenes found favour in this compilation, especially where changes have occurred in the intervening years, along with snapshots of public occasions, local worthies, obsolete machines, parades, sporting and ceremonial events and natural disasters. It is hoped that all form an interesting commentary on life in past years, alongside the brief historical sketch which prefaces each volume to help tell the story of each place, before the camera added a new dimension to the historical record.

The availability of prints has been greatly reduced by the lottery of time, leaving the final selection to be made from survivals in private hands. Local reference libraries appear not to have extended their activities into photographic archives until recently. The cupboards of newspaper offices are surprisingly bare, while the studios of professional photographers have proved eminently combustible.

The major source of the older prints of the district, taken between the 1880s and 1914, was the excellent Macintosh Collection, still preserved on glass plates. For the use of a portion of these the author is indebted to Mr George Hood of Ferndale, Galston and to Dr. J. B. Simpson of Gleniffer, Newmilns, trustee of the Auld Newmilns Collection, based largely on the work of John Macintosh of Strath Mill. Although it was not possible to reproduce all the prints made available by numerous donors, some anonymous, thanks are due to the following for their generous help in the production of this book:—

Mrs M. Allison, Mrs J. Beggs, Miss C. Black, Robert Brown, R. F. Findlay, James Frater, John Goldie, Sam Hill, Mrs C. McEwan, Miss K. McGhee, William McGregor, J. Stewart McLauchlan, Alex McNair, Ian Pollock, James Pollock, Tom Ross, Hamish Stevenson, Mrs D. Todd, Robert Todd, Mrs M. Walker, Mrs M. Woodburn, Mrs M. Young, Kilmarnock & Loudoun District Council Museum Services and the Ordnance Survey.

Newmilns
Ayrshire

J.M.
1988

HISTORICAL SKETCH

The town of Newmilns in Ayrshire is now approaching the five hundredth anniversary of its formation as a burgh of barony. During the reign of King James IV a charter was granted under the Great Seal of Scotland at Linlithgow Palace on 9th January 1490 (old style) on the supplication of George Campbell of Loudoun. This act gave official recognition, and the benefits of patronage, to the small settlement which had been developing for some time at the fording point of the River Irvine in the narrowest part of the Irvine Valley. The town's name originates in the corn mills situated on the river bank to which the farmers of Loudoun parish took their corn for grinding.

The name appears again in 1494, when Johne Campbell of New Mylnes, one of the early reformers known as the Lollards of Kyle, was summoned before the king on a charge of heresy. His home was probably on or near the site of the 16th century fortified tower house still standing in Castle Street, which later gave protection to the small number of inhabitants in the cluster of houses near its walls.

Very little growth occurred in the first century of the burgh's existence. These were turbulent times in Scotland. In 1513 James IV was killed at Flodden. His son James V died after the battle of Solway Moss in 1542, and his grand-daughter Mary was deposed and finally judicially murdered in England in 1587. The established national church was destroyed and its lands and benefices confiscated, leaving the country too unsettled to encourage the peaceful arts which the royal charter intended to promote.

Yet the charter supplied the potential for future development, granting the inhabitants full power to buy and sell "wines, wax, woolen and linen cloth, broad and narrow," and liberty to have "bakers, brewers, fleshers and sellers as well of flesh as of fish, and any other craftsmen, anyways pertaining and belonging to the freedom of a Burgh of Barony." Most of the people of the parish still lived in groups of small farms, known as ferm-touns, beyond the burgh boundary. The surnames of families living in the town between 1569 and 1572, when baptismal records were first kept, were Aird, Brown, Howie, Kirkland, Lockhart, Mospatrick, Torrance and Walker.

In 1593 the corn mill of Newmilns was leased to a James Loudoun and remained in the same family for three hundred years, becoming known latterly as Loudoun's Mill. Nearby there was also a waulk mill to full the cloth woven in the parish, providing evidence of the early organisation of the weaving trade. Before the end of the 16th century craftsmen working in the district included blacksmiths, tailors, waulkers, soutars (shoemakers), websters, wrights, millers and creelmen, (who carried goods to market in creels of their own making.)

Apart from the events connected with the struggle between church and state, there are very few local references to social or working life in the 17th century.

One of the earliest descriptions of Newmilns is by Timothy Pont, the first map-maker of Scotland along scientific lines. Around 1608, he tells of "a fair and veill bult duelling decored with plesant gardens and orchardes, it belongs to ye Lord Loudoun, having a parish churche so named with a stone bridge over ye River Irvine."

Most people still lived in the countryside, but there was a gradual increase in the number of specialist craftsmen involved in "customer trade," when orders were made up for individual families, sometimes by itinerant tailors and shoemakers in the customers own homes. Only small amounts of surplus goods were available for market due to the shortage of raw materials and the primitive techniques of manufacture. This was especially so in weaving, which was a slow and intricate operation until near the end of the century and the arrival of Huguenot and Flemish refugees from the Continent with their advanced weaving methods. Many families in the Valley trace their origins in the district back to these immigrants.

In 1633 a new parish church was built in Newmilns to replace the small and decaying pre-reformation structure at Loudoun Kirk, bringing the ecclesiastical centre into the growing town. From then until 1688 there was no respite from religious conflict. In 1638 every male head of household was required to sign the National Covenant in support of the presbyterian form of church organisation.

The Campbells of Loudoun played leading roles in the wars that followed and, as one of the services still enforced by feudal superiors, the men of the parish were pressed to take up arms. Many fought in the Scottish army under John, 1st Earl of Loudoun, during the invasion of England in 1640 and took part in the siege and subseqent occupation of Newcastle. During Cromwell's rule in Scotland, a citadel was built at Ayr to control the people of south-west Scotland. A detachment of the army under General Monk suppressed all resistance in the area and bombarded and took possession of Loudoun Castle. Until it was destroyed by fire in 1941 some of the damage done to the walls during the siege could still be seen.

James, 2nd Earl of Loudoun found favour with neither Cromwell nor Charles II after the king's Restoration. He was an exile in Holland until his death in 1684, while the parish minister John Nevay was also banished in 1662 and died abroad. Throughout the reign of Charles II and until James VII deserted the throne in 1688 the people of Newmilns and Loudoun parish were subjected to military repression. As fervent Covenanters they risked the imposition of fines for non-attendance at church, imprisonment, exile or death for refusal to accept the oath of allegiance; and summary execution if found armed and attending field conventicles. Yet, many still fought under the flag of the Covenant at the battles of Rullion Green, Drumclog and Bothwell Brig.

In the churchyard at Newmilns commemorative stones recall the names of the men of Loudoun parish killed between 1666 and 1685. Matthew Paton, shoemaker in Newmilns, was executed for being in arms at Rullion Green. David Findlay was shot on the order of General Tam Dalziel on suspicion of being with the Covenanting army. John Gebbie of Feoch, John Morton of Broomhill and Thomas Fleming of Loudoun Hill were killed at Drumclog or died later of their wounds. James Wood was executed for his appearance at Bothwell Brig, as also were John Nisbet of Glen and James Nisbet of Highside. John Law was shot by a guard when Newmilns Keep was attacked by local men and eight prisoners liberated. The old Keep was used as a prison and a billet for soldiers. It was also the headquarters of the notorious Captain Inglis whose ultimate act of barbarity was the execution and decapitation of James White in Fenwick. The Covenanter's head was carried back and put to gruesome use as a football by the soldiers on Newmilns town green. A gravestone in Fenwick tells the tale.

"This martyr was by Peter Inglis shot,
By birth a Tyger rather than a Scot,
Who that his monstrous
Extract might be seen
Cut off his head and kick't it
O'er the Green.
This was that head which
Was to wear a Crown
A football made by A profane
Dragoon."

The most illustrious Covenanter from Loudoun was John Nisbet of Hardhill who had served as a mercenary on the Continent. He had the post of captain at Bothwell Brig and was one of the last to leave the battle ground. Having also been at Rullion Green and Drumclog he was declared a rebel with 3,000 merks reward offered for his capture. Finally betrayed he was executed at the Grassmarket in Edinburgh in 1685. His farm of Hardhill lay in Loudoun manse glebe, the site of which is still marked by old foundations in a curve of the burn. It had been the home of his great-grandfather Murdoch Nisbet first translator of the New Testament into Scots.

After the struggles of the Covenanters the district settled into a long period of peace, undisturbed until a century later when the influence of the French Revolution was felt. Scottish industry recovered slowly after the Union of Parliaments in 1707, when cheaper English goods, especially in woolen products, flowed into the country. There followed an era of slow and painstaking development in trade and agriculture.

John, 4th Earl of Loudoun's military career was not enhanced under General John Cope during the 1745 Jacobite Rising, nor as Commander-in-Chief of the British army in the American colonies, but he transformed the farmland of his parish by his agricultural improvements. Described in the Old Statistical Account of Scotland as the father of agriculture in this part of Ayrshire, he planted up to a million trees between the years 1733 and 1775. He changed the old run-rig system of farming by enclosing fifty farms of twenty to fifty acres each, built a road from his castle to Newmilns, and encouraged the growing of rye-grass and clover, and of turnips for winter fodder. A number of lime kilns built to provide lime to spread on the land can still be seen on the estate. Those near Hyndberrybank bear the date 1774. He laid the foundations of the modern landscape we see on the northern flank of the Valley today — the "Loudoun's Bonnie Woods and Braes" of Robert Tannahill's song.

Alongside those changes on the land the Burgh of Newmilns was growing into an estimable little town on the strength of the expanding linen-weaving trade which coincided with the introduction of the flying shuttle. In 1739 an impressive council house was built at the Cross with a steeple, bell and double forestair, the scene of many proclamations and political harangues down the years. The burgh charter granted that the burgesses "may have, hold and possess forever a Cross and Market on Sunday weekly, and public Fairs on every year forever upon the feast day of Saint Dionisius in Autumn." Another charter conferred by Sir Matthew Campbell of Loudoun in 1566 gave the bailies and council the right to hold courts. The new Council House had an upper chamber for council and court business, and downstairs a jail with a vaulted ceiling and a small barred window.

From the 1730's onwards the town flourished, but only burgesses enjoyed the benefits of residence. They had the sole right to buy and sell at the market cross and take part in council elections. Fees of fifteen shillings were charged for burgess tickets, but these were also granted to persons who had been of service to the town. One of the honorary freemen was David Dale, cotton manufacturer and partner with Robert Owen, the great educational reformer, in the foundation of the model industrial village of New Lanark.

Others included the Rev. Mr George Lawrie and Gavin Hamilton, both friends and patrons of the poet Robert Burns. The troubled times following the French Revolution, when soldiers were quartered in the town, brought Hugh Montgomerie, Esquire, of Coilsfield, Colonel of the West Lowland Fencibles on to the burgess roll in 1793, along with all the commissioned officers of the regiment. The excess of loyalty shown by these invitations was greatly changed during the economic depression after the Napoleonic Wars, and the campaigns for parliamentary reform. We find instead the renowned radical leader William Cobbett M.P., was awarded the freedom of the burgh in 1829.

Another feature of the old burgh of barony, which had been raised to a burgh of regality in 1707, was its system of closed corporations. No one could practise his trade unless he had completed an indentured apprenticeship and been admitted to one of the incorporated trades of shoemakers, tailors, wrights or any of the other crafts active in the town. In Newmilns the weavers were the largest and most important group.

An indication of the economic health of the linen trade in the middle of the 18th Century and of the changing times was the institution of the Trades' Race in 1743. The preamble of the Trades' Race Book declares that "when mechanics become fatigued by honest industry, and their bodies languid with constant labour, some innocent amusement is absolutely necessary to exhilerate the spirits, and invigorate health. Running is an amusement of very ancient date. It was one of the Olympic games, practised in Greece, when in the zenith of her glory, and as it tends to create emulation in those who run, it also gives singular satisfaction to the spectators." Gone were the days of sterner pursuits when all able-bodied men had to practise at the bow butts in readiness for army service.

Some of the articles governing the race required that to purchase flags and sashes "every person shall pay one shilling sterling of entry money," and competitors had to be of three years residence. A later article stated that "no married man shall be elected as flag carrier." All the signs point to the days of the Trades and Town Races as the major festivals of the year, days of colourful ceremony with processions led by the town's officers and mace bearers. The final account of items in the Burgh Treasurer's Box lists five flags, one handbell, four constables batons and two brass thistles to be fixed to the top of flagpoles. Very little of the insignia or emblems of the old burgh survive, although a number of interesting relics and documents were lodged until recently in the museum in Lady Flora's Institute.

The second half of the 18th century was a period of considerable progress in the trade and prosperity of the burgh. Those were the days of the gentleman weavers. attracting into their ranks the younger sons of farmers, and of the more affluent families who could afford to apprentice their sons to master craftsmen. The trade had originated in woolen work and had expanded rapidly into linen manufacture in the 1730's and 40's. By the 1780's some silk was being woven but a decade later saw a mass movement into the production of cotton goods. In 1791 the number of weavers had increased to 241 male and 25 female, and the population was around one thousand. From that time the burgh began to take itself seriously.

The burgh's assets had been mysteriously reduced from the old five pound lands (about 250 acres) conferred in the original charters. These had extended from the river to Darnahill in the north-west and Astinpapple in the north-east. The alienation of these lands over the centuries could suggest corruption in the council, but might more charitably be put down to their sale to carry the council over difficult times. The property still in burghal hands was an area at Bridgend, the West and East Strands, Blackton Yard and Green Road, the Cross and the Green.

Items listed in the council inventory included a translation of the original charter of 1490; a charter in Latin granted by Sir Matthew Campbell of Loudoun in 1566; an obligation by the Earl of Loudoun to the town of Newmilns anent the Tolbooth and Council Chamber; the town records; the copper plate for printing burgess tickets; one iron stamp; one set of jougs for punishing malefactors; one large padlock for the Tolbooth; two causeway hammers for repairing the causeway; and copies of the acts of Parliament from James VI to Charles II. There were also the imperial weights and measures in the hands of the Troner, Mr James Boyd, essential to ensure fair dealing at the Tron, the public weighing machine, which was erected at the Cross on market days.

The emoluments of office were as common then as now. In the Treasurer's Accounts we find:
"To spending at Charles Campbell's Inn at the Foot Race ... 3s 1d."
Not only the runners worked up a thirst "Expenses at the Bailies choosing...9s 3d". This seems an excessively large amount for election refreshments when we discover that further on "selling ground at the last corner of the churchyard" brought in only £3. However, innovation and enterprise traditionally associated with Newmilns is evident in the purchase of

lamps in 1823 for the earliest street illumination. The bill for these was reckoned:
"By cash to John Lawson for lamps.... £15 5s 11½d.
By cash to Wm. King assisting putting them up .... 5/-.

By cash to Alexander Peden for leather for lamps, lamp posts, wicks and 34 pints of oil.... 5/-."

The guarding and nourishing of prisoners also fell on the public purse. In 1824 the following entries were made:
"By cash to Hugh Smith for bread for Roxburgh and other prisoners and for the guard.... 3/-.
By cash to John Morton, porter (ale) for prisoner and guard.... 6/-.
By cash for Alex Pollock for straw for prisoners.... 3d."

The inner as well as the outer comfort of inmates received attention and they seem to have dined with their guards. It was around this time the following piece of doggerel was found scrawled on the wall of the jail after an unhappy prisoner had been released.

"In the coonty of Ayr
   Between twa hills,
Lies the auld burgh toon
   O' Newmilns.
It boasts of a steeple
   And an auld gothic cell,
Twa rotten bailies
   An an auld crackit bell."

Although the town had prospered between 1730 and 1815 on the growth of the weaving trade, there were also hard times which led to unrest and the constant use of the town jail. Meal riots were common following poor harvests. In 1800 farmers in Loudoun parish were warned not to allow meal out of the district, or to charge extra for it, or, as a handbill threatened "your house shall burn at least." In the same year carts of meal bound for Strathaven were confiscated. One was taken to Newmilns and left in the street for the townswomen to come and plunder it. The magistrates had difficulty keeping order in the town in the early part of last century. There were two squads of young men known as the Imperials and the Keelies who "kept the whole parish in an uproar" and were "terrors to the peaceful inhabitants all around Newmilns." As late as 1836 in the Treasurer's Accounts there is an entry:
"By cash to magistrates at enquiry about the battle in the church yard.... 1/-."
Also:
"Expense for three boys, three days in jail.... 3s 4½d."

The suffering of the destitute before the introduction of the new Scottish Poor Law in 1845 can be seen from the following entries.
In 1837
"Paid to travellers in distress with passports .... 4s 6d."
"To a poor woman in distress.... 6d."
The poor could not move from one parish to another without a passport as the authorities feared they would become a burden on church poor funds, so in 1839 we find
"Paid for a cart for returning a beggar to Galston.... 1s 6d"

In the same year an item shows the council in advance of its time by employing a dog-catcher.
"To John Steel for keeping dogs from the street....
                                                          1s 6d."
Perhaps he was related to Lilias Steel, another council employee who was paid three shillings in 1836 "for cleaning the jail twice and washing the Band Room."

By that date the town had witnessed wide swings of fortune. Weaving was still the staple industry, but the days of the gentleman weaver were gone forever. In 1792 the best weavers had been able to earn four shillings a day. An account of their most successful times tells how "they only wrought three days a week, and those disposed betook themselves to the change house for the next three days. Here a flaffer (a pound) was pinned to the partition wall, which when 'melted' was taken down by the landlord, just to be replaced by another." Inspired by the French Revolution and the book "The Rights of Man," by Tom Paine, weavers in the district formed themselves into Societies of the Friends of the People. Led by Thomas Muir of Huntershill, working men called for measures of parliamentary reform, but these were denied and the movement was crushed by the government.

When the Napoleonic Wars ended in 1815 the burgh entered its deepest economic depression. Various factors caused this. Many ex-soldiers flooded the labour market and control of entry to the trade by the master weavers was lost. Power looms were increasing in number, producing plain goods at cheaper rates. If a weaver was lucky enough to have a web to weave his wages were little over four shillings a week. Whereas in 1792 leisure hours and democratic principles had stimulated a desire for reform, by 1819 poverty and deprivation had fired a new radical movement.

Newmilns was a centre for the mass demonstrations held in the west of Scotland. One was held on the Town Green on 7 September 1819, attended by four thousand people "for the purpose of taking into consideration the distressed state of the country and the best remedy for its relief." Nicol Brown of Lanfine, a Depute Lieutenant of Ayrshire, reported to his superior Lord Eglinton how insecure the civil authorities felt and complained that it would take three hours to summon troops from Kilmarnock. It proved difficult to swear in special constables, but forty finally enrolled, mostly farmers and millers, while another ten refused to turn out to attend the next demonstration on 25 September.
    They were:
    William Dalglish, Allanton,
    Thos Morton Jun., Ladybrow,

Francis Findlay, Dalloy,
James Mitchell, Dyke,
Alex Mair, Parkerston,
William Torrance, Gatehouse,
Hugh Woodburn, Mains,
John Woodburn, Mains,
John Morton, Broomhill,
Andrew Morton, Broomhill.

Over three thousand appeared at this demonstration and Brown told Eglinton that as arranged "Neither drums or music were used in going to the meeting. It was observed, however, that a great number were furnished with powerful sticks. But when they broke up they paraded along the street passing in front of the Inn, where the magistrates were assembled, making a very formidable appearance, altho they could not but know that such was in defiance of their express orders." These, with similar events elsewhere, were the early stages of the Radical War, which led up to open rebellion in the Spring of 1820. On the first day of April a proclamation was posted up in all the weaving centres, calling for the establishment of a Provisional Government. It is now thought to have been the work of government agents, attempting to bring about a premature rising. The weavers in Newmilns had earlier been requested to keep men who had enlisted in the yeomanry under surveillance. When the signal came they were to go to their homes, disarm them and take possession of their weapons.

At one of the meetings on the Green a line was drawn on the ground by a weaver named Cuthill, who issued a challenge that "all those who will march in the cause of liberty had to cross." In preparation some were seen to sharpen "their pikes at Scouller's hone" at Pate's Mill. On the 2nd April the Ayrshire Yeomanry received orders to march on Glasgow and Paisley. The men of Loudoun and Galston parishes set out on the 3rd but a number refused to answer the call and their names were attached by Brown of Lanfine to a list of those to be dealt with later for questionable allegiance. After two weeks the Edinburgh Yeomanry arrived on their "Western Campaign" and on 14th April occupied Kilmarnock, Strathaven and Newmilns. Earlier the general rising had collapsed at the battle of Bonnymuir with the subsequent execution of leaders Baird, Hardie and Wilson and the transportation to Australia of many others.

In Newmilns men had met, sensed a plot, and quickly disbanded but under the direction of Nicol Brown a search was made for the radicals who had been seen in arms. A number escaped to America, while others skulked in the neighbourhood like their Covenanting forefathers and were helped by the people to escape capture until, with the intercession of the same Nicol Brown of Lanfine, they were finally pardoned at the coronation of George IV.

The first Reform Bill was passed in 1832. This allowed 98 males to vote in Loudoun Parish when previously they had numbered only three. Such a limited extension of the franchise still left the vast majority of people without a vote. The radical spirit of the weavers was transferred into the new, nationwide Chartist Movement with the people of Loudoun again pressing for the use of physical force to achieve a democratic parliamentary system. Once more their hopes were dashed. The government frustrated all the aims of the Charter and by 1848 the movement had disintegrated and a number of men found themselves again in hiding or forced to escape to America.

Meanwhile the handloom weaving trade was in transition. All over the country weavers were replaced by power-loom operatives, except in areas where fine goods were produced. In the Irvine Valley the weavers specialised in figured muslin, first on the lappet loom, which could put a simple spot or decoration on the cloth, and then on the jacquard loom which was capable of an all-over design. The final period of prosperity for the local handloom weavers lasted for thirty-five years from 1838. This was the year in which a young joiner and wright, Joseph Hood, introduced the first jacquard machine to the Valley. The weavers in the district were soon flocking to the Hoods and the Mitchells for the new style looms, bought on hire purchase. One of the attractions of the jacquard was that it did away with the need for draw-boys; children of eight years and upwards who had been required to draw the combination of strings before every shot to determine the pattern in the weave. Often the tediousness of the job turned these youngsters, who were supposed to be servants of their masters, into virtual dictators. As young girls from the same age were engaged as hand clippers, education in the town could make no real advance until mechanical means were found to release children from these tasks.

Within a few years the whole district had built up a thriving trade and extensive reputation for book and leno curtains which sustained it into the 1870s. While in other areas numbers declined, in Newmilns they rose from 550 handloom weavers in 1842 to 952 in 1872. The system of production stemmed from manufacturers in Glasgow and Paisley who despatched the webs to their agents in the Valley, known as "Wee Corks." They in turn issued the webs to their weavers who worked at home on their handlooms, and also gave out the yarn for pirn winding which was done by the women and girls in the weaving families. When the cloth was woven it was returned to the agents wa'room (ware room) where it was carefully checked for quality and faults before payment was made. As Thomas Bruce one of the many Newmilns rhymers described it;
"Doun gaed their glesses on his claith,
   Where'er a shot seemed missin,
Wi stoppages they were na laith
   His sma' returns to lessen."

The agents then prepared their loads of finished cloth for the carrier, who would bring his horse and cart to selected parts of the town and call out "ocht or nocht for Glesca" A number of carriers augmented their incomes, with the overnight haul of local poachers. It was a hazardous journey. Matthew Mair, one of the Newmilns carriers, was robbed of £400 on his way back from Glasgow, with agents money to pay the weavers, and left for dead on his cart. Luckily the horse moved on to the next stopping place where it was usually fed and the carrier was found unconscious. Also a weaver known only in story as Jenny Ge's man, after carrying his web into the city, disappeared without trace while returning on the weavers' road between Myres Farm and High Overmuir.

Practically the whole population of the town was dependent on handloom weaving in 1842. These were listed as:
 Male weavers 460
 Female weavers 90
 Clippers 230
 Winders of Pirns 154
 Weavers' wrights 8
 Warpers, warpwinders and starchers 12
 Mounters and twisters 4
 Agents and manufacturers 13

Clipping, the cutting of the floating threads from the cloth to produce the pattern, was done exclusively by women and girls, until the Clipping Mill was built in Brown Street in mid century. Mounters and twisters were specialists who entered warps in looms. A mount was a new warp and a twist a continuation of an existing one. One of the customs for a weaver out of work for some time was to receive "a kick" from an agent. This was the name for an advance in cash to finance a new web in his loom, paying for the services of a mounter, a heddle-caster and a card cutter.

When the Reverend Norman MacLeod was parish minister in Loudoun he wrote many accounts of life in the town between 1838 and 1845. His novel "The Starling" still gives a strong impression of the Calvinist background, but passages in his letters provide a less sentimental description of what he found. On his arrival he discovered "a set of shrewd, well-read, philosophical weavers..., vain: but marvellously well informed, and half infidel — who were very civil when I went to see them, but would never come to church. They were generally Chartists and talked very big about the 'priests' not wishing the people to become well-informed." The Chartists had at that time a majority in the council. They also maintained a Chartist Provision Store with 248 members, but it declined with the Chartist movement, to reappear in 1856 as the Co-operative Society. Other mutual benefit groups of a social and educational nature included a masonic lodge dating from 1747, a savings bank, a funeral society and a farmers' fire insurance scheme. There were also a town band dating from 1833, a philosophical institution, and a subscription library.

Before the evangelism of the Temperance Movement swept the country after mid-century, there were fifteen public houses or hotels in the town. Perhaps cotton fluff caused as great a drouth as coal dust, for Newmilns weavers rivalled Galston miners in their convivial pursuits. Some of these public houses survive today, while others have changed their names, but the Treddle Hole east of the parish church is long gone with the handloom weavers who frequented it, along with the Bowit Brace quaintly named after its cracked fireplace. The darker side of life in the town is described by Norman MacLeod. "Families will live for days, and even weeks, on a few potatoes and salt, before they seek public aid." And when prices fell for handloom goods many turned to the whisky shop. "A weaver after sitting sixteen hours a day in a damp loom shop, without healthy bodily exercise, his nerves unstrung, his digestive organs deranged will often rob himself of food and raiment to banish, by intoxication, the bodily wretchedness and mental irritability which he knows from sad experience, will soon return with increased misery." There was also a problem with youth at the time. "Much whisky is consumed in our villages by a class of weavers called 'trampers,' generally young men, who, wearied of the restrictions of the home, wander from village to village, working for such as keep looms on purpose to supply those wandering mechanics. They live miserably, spending the greater portion of their wages in whisky, which they consume, not only in public and private houses, but also in the fields."

The powers and functions of the old council began to be superseded when Newmilns became a Police Burgh in 1834. From that date onwards there were two rival councils in the town. The council of the old burgh of barony jealous of their position refused to accept the upstart new council for over seventy years. They continued to sit in the Council Chamber at the Cross, levying customs, collecting dues, granting burgess tickets and falling out with the new council, whenever they felt their privileges were infringed. Expenses were chiefly incurred in the upkeep of the Council House and Tolbooth, in the elections and in choosing the bailies, maintenance of the town clock, the bell and drum. Five shillings were paid annually to the two officers for shoes, the halberds were cleaned regularly, the weights at the tron were inspected and replaced when necessary and the street lamps kept in oil and wicks. Prizes were given at the races and the drummer and pikemen provided with ribbons and sashes, all to perpetuate the pride and distinction of a council created in antiquity by royal charter.

In 1872 the Police Burgh boundaries were extended over the river Irvine into Galston parish creating the larger burgh of Newmilns and Greenholm. At the beginning of the 20th century new and comprehensive powers given to the council led a correspondent to the local newspaper to comment that "no rational being would ever think of paying the Old Town Council 8/6d to be made one. The Act of 1901 makes every man a burgess who has paid his rates for three years." The old council had refused to lie down.

In July 1894 the burgesses and councillors visited Loudoun Moor to assert their rights to cut peat, given by Sir Matthew Campbell of Loudoun in 1566. His charter granted "free access and entry in and to the lands, moors and marches by use and wont, pertaining or which may be justly held to pertain to the bailies, inhabitants and future inhabitants of the said burgh in all time to come."

When they reached West Heads farm there was a policeman at the gate on the road leading to the moor, and on coming on to the moss were met by Mr Hendrie, factor to Lord Donington, and two gamekeepers. Mr William Steel, Chancellor of the Council, invited the factor and the others on to a bank of heather, where he read out the appropriate parts of the charter, and then cut a peat in the name of the burgh and inhabitants of Newmilns. In a short speech the Chancellor regretted the change which had come over relations between the House of Loudoun and the Burgh of Newmilns. The company then gave three hearty cheers to the memory of those old lords of the manor who had been so friendly to the inhabitants of the town in olden times, and had sworn to defend the burgh, its privileges and liberties. Shortly after this little ceremony the relevant charter was "mislaid" and has not yet reappeared, proving the good sense of those Scottish Border towns who put no faith in pieces of paper and ride their marches every year.

The townspeople had not been able to repeat the triumph of a year earlier when they had won a famous right-of-way case in the Court of Session. Fences and gates had been erected across the Lime Road at the Hag Brig in 1870, 1878, 1886 and 1891 and quickly demolished by the weavers. The case was pursued by one of their number Hugh Smith against Lord Donington, and the evidence of some of the witnesses gives an insight into life in the town at that time. Hugh Alexander said "the weavers were their own masters, and worked what hours they liked. They did not work much on a Monday, nor a pay day. On the latter day, as soon as they got paid in the afternoon, they went for a walk."

The substantial fences across the road were systematically destroyed with saws and axes until, with the final decision in favour of Hugh Smith, the path through the Bluebell Planting from the Hag Brig to Woodhead farm was, from 1893, once again accessible to all.

Within two decades a dramatic change occured in the lifestyle of the town's people. The collapse of handloom weaving prices in 1872 struck the final blow. From that date there was a rapid drop in the number of weavers from 952 to barely a score by the end of the century. They had gone on their last strike as the manufacturers cut prices, but other related factors lay in the technical advance of the power-loom, able to copy the most intricate handloom designs, while leno goods were undercut by the curtains made on the Nottingham lace machines. The weavers were further humiliated when their union officers had their household goods auctioned at the Cross to meet unpaid fines incurred when they refused admission to non-striking members to the Beaming House to warp their beams.

The end of handloom weaving coincided with the final years of the old council of the Burgh of Barony. Just as a few old weavers stubbornly remained at their looms for another thirty years, the old council continued to sit, while their powers were eroded by the new Police Burgh of Newmilns and Greenholm.

However, in 1876 a new trade had been introduced which carried the town forward for another seventy prosperous years. Joseph Hood, mechanic, and Hugh Morton, weaving agent, followed the lead of Alexander Morton of Darvel, and installed the first lace curtain machine in their wincey mill in Greenholm. Within ten years there were a further eight companies formed with work for over 1500 employees, and with a large complement of lace, madras and lappet machines in operation.

People came flooding back to the town, to take up the opportunities in the lace factories; all being skilled in "reading the flower," that is, in being able to tell from textile experience that the pattern of the cloth was correct in the machine.

The old handloom terms survived in the new lace operation. Few of the Nottingham ones were adopted in Scotland. A lace machine is a loom, a twisthand is a weaver, a brass bobbin with its carriage is a shuttle, ties are shots, to tie-in is to heddle-in, the depression for the warp beam is the treddle hole, and a fault in the cloth usually meant that something was "aff the shot."

In the mid 1870s grass had been growing in the streets. By the mid 1880s there was a senior football team in the town, the burgh band had been re-revived after a lapse of some years, and Brown's Institute built in 1870 was soon a hive of activity used by innumerable local groups, including Good Templars, Rachebites, Loudoun Choral Society, Plymouth Brethren, Salvation Army and Hugh Morton's Young Men's Sabbath Morning Class.

The Co-operative Society's public meetings were held there as well as most of the town's weddings and annual socials. The Morton Hall and the Co-operative Hall did not take over these functions until their construction in 1894 and 1900 respectively, but the Institute remained as the communal centre with its reading and games rooms. In 1904 the summer ice tables were replaced by billiards and a new craze overwhelmed the youth of the town. Some thought this innovation dangerous to morals and that the Institute had become nothing more than a gambling den and billiards "a sure way to show the young men of Newmilns who frequented it a quick road to perdition."

Despite prophesies of doom at the millennium, the town entered the 20th century with an air of prosperity which permeated every aspect of public life. Social, athletic and cultural activities proliferated, the lace industry was booming and the council of Newmilns and Greenholm indulged in so many new enterprises the burgh became known as The Town of Light and Leading. The 1st World War was soon to throw a blight on the life of the community, but, with the end of the excessive thraldom of work suffered by earlier generations, the 20th century also brought the advances and opportunities, which placed the people in a position to face contemporary challenges, as the town approached the end of the fifth century of its corporate existence.

Newmilns had come into existence in 1490 as little more than a name on a document, granted to encourage the tenants of a few corn mills and a group of houses to develop into a burgh with trading privileges. Over the next three hundred years it grew slowly but was still contained within a small area bounded by the present Main Street, with additional houses in Greenside and down East and West Strands to the fords across the river.

With the success of the handloom weaving trade in cotton goods, from the late 18th century into the third quarter of the 19th century, further extensions were made into Union Street, Kilnholm Street, King Street, High Street and Drygate Street, with additional expansion across the river into Greenholm on feus granted by the Browns of Lanfine in Brown Street and Nelson Street.

It was not until after the introduction of the lace industry in 1876 that Newmilns exploded beyond its old boundaries. The population jumped to over 4,000 at the beginning of the century and was approaching 5,000 before the 1st World War. The feeling of confidence at that period can hardly be imagined. New factories and streets of houses seemed to spring up overnight. Kilnholm Street continued into Loudoun Road, with the villas of the new manufacturing and managerial class at the west end. Buildings of a similar type appeared in Darvel Road and up Borebrae, while vacant ground, not already occupied by the lace mills which monopolised the level sites, were quickly filled up with houses some of which clung precariously to the hillsides as at Baldie's Brae, Drygatehead and Campbell Street.

The impressive Co-operative Buildings, Lady Flora's School and the new school in High Street, the Morton Hall and Brown's Institute, with the already established churches, added substance to the impression of a community with a thriving commercial life. The comparatively high standard of living of the people engaged in the lace industry, and the attractive location of the town, created in the citizens of Newmilns and its exiles abroad an affectionate attachment to the place of their birth.

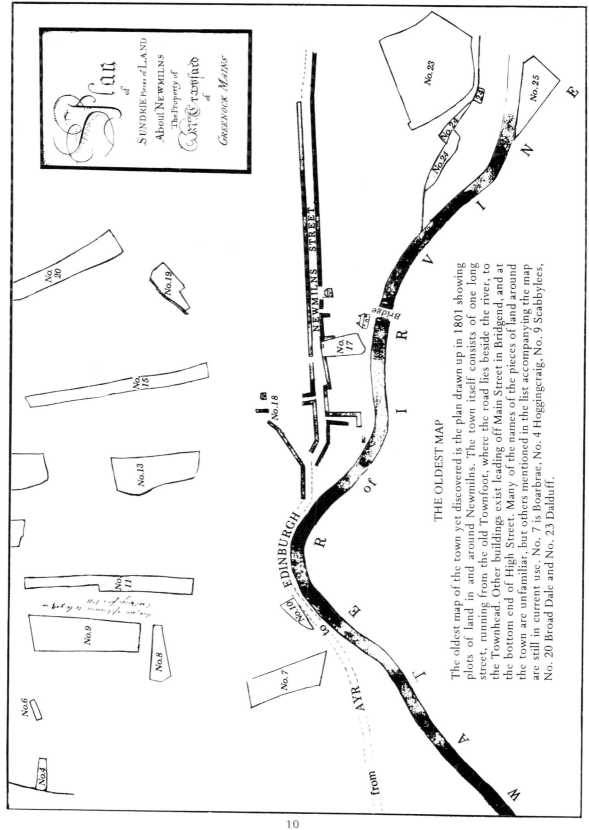

THE OLDEST MAP

The oldest map of the town yet discovered is the plan drawn up in 1801 showing plots of land in and around Newmilns. The town itself consists of one long street, running from the old Townfoot, where the road lies beside the river, to the Townhead. Other buildings exist leading off Main Street in Bridgend, and at the bottom end of High Street. Many of the names of the pieces of land around the town are unfamiliar, but others mentioned in the list accompanying the map are still in current use. No. 7 is Boarbrae, No. 4 Hoggingcraig, No. 9 Scabbylees, No. 20 Broad Dale and No. 23 Dalduff.

LOUDOUN PARISH KIRK

Built in 1844 is seen here in an old print from around 1850. It replaced an earlier church, dating from 1738. The new church was erected over the old, which was then demolished and the stone used in the construction of some of the cottages in High Street. The first church on the site was established in 1633, when the congregation moved from Loudoun Kirk to the main centre of population in the expanding burgh of Newmilns. Also seen are the town's Green with the open Norrel Burn running across it to the River Irvine, and the fine, new, stone bridge crossing to Browns Road.

THE KEEP

The oldest building in the town is the fortified tower house in the New Road (now Castle Street), seen here in 1892 soon after it was re-roofed. Of considerable architectural and historical interest it was maintained in good condition for many years by the owners of the adjacent Loudoun Arms Hotel. Built in the 16th Century, it was in the possession of John Campbell of Newmilns, who was summoned before King James IV as one of the early church reformers known as the Lollards of Kyle. In 1685 while being used as barracks for dragoons and as a prison, it was attacked by local men who released eight Covenanter prisoners. Since then it has been used as a grain store, a doocot, a band hall and a beer cellar. Although a B listed building, and under the protection of local and national government, it is now sadly neglected.

AULD NEWMILNS in 1894

Looking towards Lanfine Woods before the railway was built to Darvel in 1896. The view is from the top of Jacob's Ladder, a right-of-way which led from Baldie's Brae to Loudoun Crescent, used regularly until the early 1970's. The burgh at this time was in its heyday as a textile manufacturing centre. Careful study will reveal the changes over the past ninety years, mainly at the old Townfoot, now known as the Co-operative Corner, and among the handloom weavers' cottages in Nelson Street on the far side of the river. In the field beside Jacob's Ladder signs of limestone workings can still be seen, although the remains of the limekilns, from which Kilnholm Street took its name, can no longer be located.

WINCEY MILL

Taken in the 1880's this was the first power-loom factory in the Valley using a steam engine. It was built in 1867 for the manufacture of wincey goods. a mixture of cotton warp and woolen weft. Partners in the enterprise were Joseph Hood, loom builder and Hugh Morton, weaving agent. It stood on an open-field site in Greenholm, preceding all the other lace and madras mills built on feus acquired from the Browns of Lanfine. The view is looking east from the rear of Pate's Mill. It was later extended for the production of lace, madras, chenille and tapestry.

THE CROSS

The scene is very little changed from the time of this photograph in the 1890's. The oldest part of the town was built near the castle, around the mercat cross. The old Council House on the left was built in 1739, during the prosperous days of the handloom linen trade. The upper apartment was used as a council room, with the jail below. On the right is the Clydesdale Bank, formerly the Black Bull Hotel. with the Loudoun Arms, formerly The Eagle Inn, at the other side of the entrance to Castle Street. A baker's apprentice is happy to pose beside the handcart used for deliveries from Andrew Smith's bakeshop.

THE LONG ENTRY

The Long Entry emerges on the Main Street beyond the sign of Dr. Aird's surgery. It led back past a number of premises to Back Street (now King Street). The pole advertises a barber who also provided baths, hot and cold, at 3d, 4d and 6d. The first shop on the left is owned by Matthew Morton. butcher. The next along is James Loudoun, baker, with his delivery van at the door.

WINDOW DISPLAY

The promotion of a particular product kept shopkeepers busy ringing the changes in their windows. In this case soap is the theme, and Lux, Swan, Sunlight and Lifebuoy are presented to the public. The window in Main Street forms part of the shop of the old-established business of James Wyllie, grocer and spirit dealer, (later belonging to James Morris), as it appeared one day in the 1890's.

THE BUTCHER'S

Matthew Morton had his shop in Main Street in a building where there is now a small public garden at the corner of East Strand. It may not seem to modern eyes the most attractive source of butcher meat, but it was fresh from animals recently killed at the local slaughter-house in King Street. A porter of the Glasgow and South Western Railway Company, on his parcel delivery round, can be seen with Mr. Morton in this photograph from the 1890's.

ROXBURGH'S SHOP

A number of grocers combined the business of grain and provision merchants, such as John Roxburgh at the corner of Main Street and Craigview Road. At this time in the 1890's, farmers had many connections with the town, having business with the shops and seed merchants, the slaughter house and the railway station. The door at the corner is now built up and the shop converted into the offices of the Scottish Lace and Window Furnishing Association.

MAIN STREET

Looking east from the corner of East Strand the street is greatly changed. On the right the range of 18th century buildings was swept away in the 1960's for a group of council houses. On the left the building with Mitchell's shoe shop and the Commercial Hotel (now the Covenanters Hotel) are all that remain. Between the Commercial Hotel and the two-storey thatched house beyond was Boose's Close (later known as the Polisman's Close), which led to Boose's Yard. All the thatched houses up to the grounds of Lady Flora's were demolished to be replaced by the Morton Hall. In the house opposite Boose's Close, Robert Tannahill the Paisley poet and composer of "Loudoun's Bonnie Woods and Braes," lodged while in the town.

A TEA SHOP

At a time when large numbers travelled into the town to work in the lace mills, small provision shops also offered meals at mid-day. Now known as cafes, they were then refreshment rooms. This one stood opposite the head of East Strand to the east of the Sun Inn (later Wyllie's Grocer Shop). As in other parts of the Main Street the entry on the right of the shop window led to a dwelling house at the rear.

THE SWEETIE SHOP

Directly opposite the Parish Church were two thatched cottages. At number 95 (now 105) was one of the innumerable sweetie shops spread throughout the town. Although the owners' chief merchandise was chocolate and sweets there was no limit on the type of goods sold and they contrived to sell everything from "dolls' een tae smiddy ashes."

THE LOUDOUN ARMS

The Loudoun Arms inn is the finest 18th century building still standing, recalling the days when Newmilns was experiencing its first period of prosperity, based on the handloom weaving industry, and its success as a small market town. The inn holds the interest of visitors with an eye for the best in the domestic architecture of Scotland. Above the door is a large painting of the coat-of-arms of the Campbells of Loudoun. Next door on Main Street is the Burns Tavern, and next again Poli's ice-cream parlour. At the end of the street is a hoarding, set up during the construction of the new Co-operative premises at the end of last century.

THE AULD COONCIL HOOSE

The auld cooncil hoose on the left was built by the feudal superior, John 4th Earl of Loudoun in 1739 to house the governing body of the Burgh of Barony. This comprised a chancellor, two bailies, a treasurer, a fiscal and thirteen councillors who sat in the upper chamber, with the tolbooth below. The old council continued to act into the 20th century, long after the Police Burgh of Newmilns and Greenholm, with its greater powers and resources, had superseded it. Not only were there two town councils. For a while there were also two gas companies. The gas lamp on the council house, like the others in the town, was supplied by the New Gas Company from its works in Hillside Place. Established in 1872, it competed with the old company situated in the area which became the town's yard, off King Street. There was a long and acrimonious battle in the 1870's before the modern plant of the new, proving more efficient, ousted the old.

> **At the Burgh of Newmilns**
> the *Fourth* day of *October* one thousand *eight* hundred and *thirty four* Years which day in Presence of Mess *John Hood* and *John Loudoun* present Baillies of said Burgh *James Morton* Treasurer thereof *Robt Morton* and *John Mair* together with the remanent Members of the Town Council Mr *Thomas Young weaver Newmilns* was entered and made a Burgess of said Burgh and had all the Liberties Privileges and Immunities thereof conferred on him in ample Form having made Oath of Fidelity as Use is In Evidence whereof these Presents extracted forth of the Court Books of said Burgh are subscribed by
>
> *James Morton Treasurer*

BURGESS TICKET

A copperplate was held in the possession of the Treasurer of the old Burgh to print and issue certificates to those made burgesses of the town. To persons with no claim to the privilege the fee was fifteen shillings, (a week's wage early last century). Reduced fees of seven shillings and sixpence were granted to sons of burgesses, with five shillings to old soldiers. Once on the roll a burgess among other perquisites had the right to vote for candidates in council elections. The copy of the ticket shown was for the year 1834, issued to Thomas Young, weaver in Newmilns.

CONSCRIPTION (Old Style)

After the outbreak of war with France in 1793, bringing a fear of invasion, a form of conscription for men between the ages of 19 and 23 was introduced by the Scottish Militia Act of 1797. It was a very unpopular measure. It led to riots in many towns and the confiscation and destruction of the baptismal registers of the churches, where the ages of candidates could be verified. The names of those eligible were balloted to serve in the Militia, but a person could escape for a time if he could afford to pay a substitute and persuade him to stand in his place. In this case Thomas Young has proposed David Orr, probably an unemployed, young weaver, as his substitute in April, 1820 at the time of the Radical War.

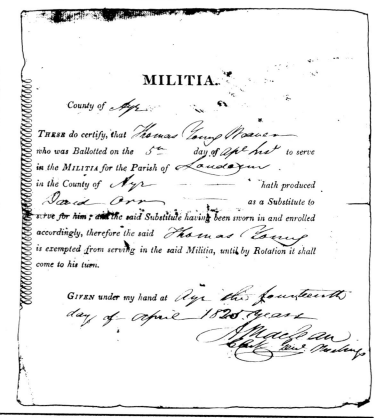

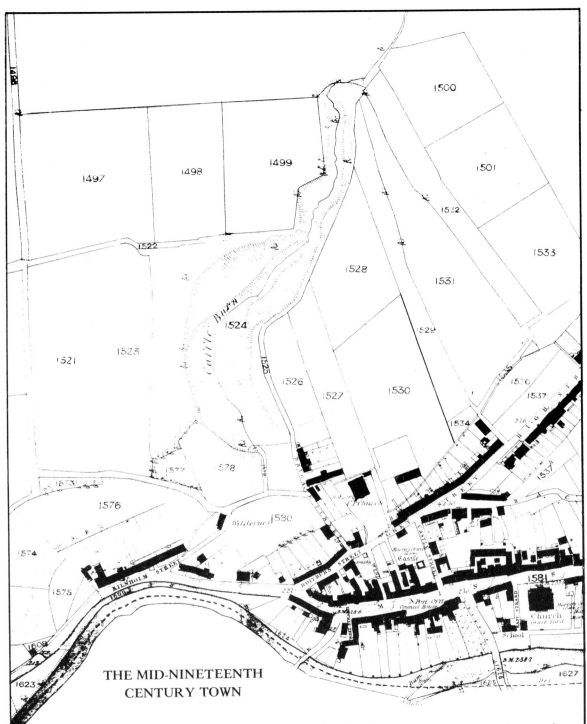

THE MID-NINETEENTH CENTURY TOWN

This map dates from 1862 when the town was at the height of success as a producer of fine, muslin, handloom goods. Many of the old names still used in conversation, have dropped out of the official record. West Strand is clearly marked leading to the old river ford at Bridgend. The Wilderness is an open field and Doitburn and Grey Streets have not been incorporated in High Street. New houses have been built further west in Kilnholm Street, with the small Toll House out on its own. There are no houses in Hillside Place and only half of Union Street is completed. The old gas works is operating behind Back Street and the Norrel Burn lies open all the way through the town and across The Green.

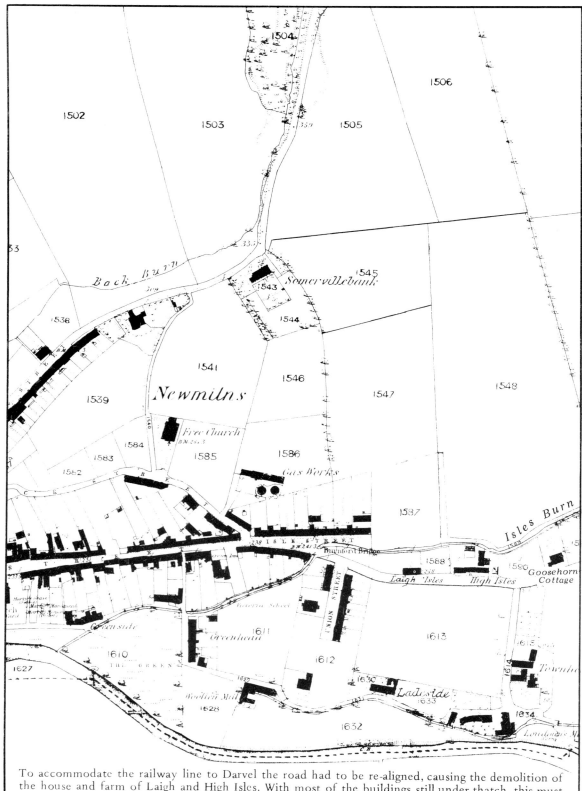

To accommodate the railway line to Darvel the road had to be re-aligned, causing the demolition of the house and farm of Laigh and High Isles. With most of the buildings still under thatch, this must have been the most pituresque period in the appearance of the town.

HOOD'S WORKSHOP

Hood's Workshop seen here in the 1890's in one of the best prints from the Macintosh Collection of photographs. This view is looking west from the entrance gates to Lady Flora's School. Straight ahead a house appears to block the road, but this was characteristic of the old town, of which it was said that houses were built where the stones were tumbled from the carts. On the left a handloom weaver with rolled white brattie or apron has come out from his loomstead for a breath of air. Behind him was Newmilns Temperance Hotel. The wooden structure is the entrance to the workshop of Joseph Hood, engineer and handloom-builder, with the timber-drying store on the upper level.

THE LIME ROAD

The Lime Road was the most popular walk of the handloom weavers. Sitting cramped at the loom all day made this particular walk from the town to the Hag Brig, through the trees to Woodhead Farm and home again their favourite form of relaxation. Baron Donington of Loudoun Castle placed strong barriers across the road from 1878 until 1893. The weavers continually tore them down, until they won their right-of-way case, on appeal, to the Court of Session. The photograph taken after the court decision shows the attraction of the road for young and old. .

A GREAT EVENT

William Morton, boot and shoe manufacturer of Birmingham, and senior partner of William Morton & Co., Lace Manufacturers, Newmilns, laying the foundation stone of the Morton Hall, on 4th April, 1896. It symbolised the new prosperity which arrived with the lace trade, and was rapidly replacing the domestic handloom weaving industry. The whole population appears to have turned out for the occasion.

MORTON HALL

The thatched cottages around Boose's Yard east of the Commercial Hotel were demolished to make room for the Morton Hall. One of the cottages was reputed to be the early home of William Morton who gifted the hall to the people of the town. It is seen here in all its pristine glory soon after completion. Outside the door to the burgh council chamber, and the public entrance are two elegant lamp standards, bearing the burgh coat-of-arms, demonstrating civic dignity and a justifiable pride of place by the inhabitants.

THE COMMERCIAL HOTEL

In the middle years of last century Glasgow manufacturers sent large amounts of muslin goods to the Valley clipping mills, and there was a huge export of textiles from the towns. A modern hotel was essential to accommodate the growing number of business visitors. In 1869 the Commercial, seen on the left, was built for this purpose. Main Street, once known as High Street, had been a continuous row of thatched cottages on both sides of the road, apart from the area of the churchyard. By mid-century more substantial dressed stone and slate roof houses were taking their place. The facade of the hotel remained as seen here for a century, before it was replaced by a mock-tudor frontage.

THE ANGEL INN

The Wilson family were the owners of this Inn shown here at the turn of the century. John Wilson stands with members of his family at the front entrance, taken from the Crown Hotel Yard opposite. Only two public houses remain on the north side of Main Street, when last century a visitor travelling east might call at five others, the Burns Tavern, Loudoun Arms, Black Bull, Cross Keys, Sun Inn and Commercial Hotel before reaching the Angel. When prohibition came to the town it lasted only a year between polls, proving ineffective as the short distance to still "wet" Galston cost only the extra price of a little shoe leather.

HORSE AND CART

The end of the 19th century and the beginning of the 20th century were the great days of the heavy horse. In the towns and countryside the pace of life was set by the speed of the work-horse. The view here in the 1890's is of the east end of Main Street with the normal complement of delivery carts and vans in any thoroughfare, during a working day. It is taken from Clark's Pend where, at the adjacent grocer's shop the local savings bank was established. The Crown Hotel can be seen on the right, in front of the projecting gable of Auld's Dairy (now Gilmour's). Looking into Isles Street the Angel Inn is on the left.

ANGEL INN CORNER

The town council before and after the second World War adopted a policy of road widening, which sealed the fate of buildings out of alignment in Main Street and at corners. The famous Angel Inn at the corner of Main Street and King Street, was also a victim of town improvements prior to the second World War. The Angel Inn had a quaintly named Athletic Bar which was the first and last call for refreshments for those attending the football matches at Hillhead Park, above Astinpapple. A small industrial area lay between the Angel Inn and Lady Flora's which included Miss Todd's hosiery, McPherson's Mercury Gas Co., and Loudoun Springs lemonade factory, in addition to the usual handloom weaving shops.

COTTAGE AND SHOP
The traditional type of handloom weaver's cottage common to the three towns of the Irvine Valley is seen in this print from the 1890's. It stood between Neil's Smiddy and Rundle's Buildings in Isles Street. Its double windows on the right point to the utilization of the interior as a two-loom workshop. By this time at the end of the handloom weaving era it had been converted into a small grocer's shop, belong to Mr. & Mrs. Lawson. Many of the weavers were too old to start afresh in the lace industry, or too independent to submit to the regimentation of factory life.

THE CROSS KEYS INN
Only the central building survives today in the photograph taken at the end of last century. At the far side was Allan McPherson's plumber's shop and at the near side Bella McPherson's draper's shop. The Cross Keys Inn was owned at the time by John Lennox, but was converted into shops and dwelling houses and the thatch removed, until it was demolished in 1939 to make way for the Rex Cinema.

A STREET PROCESSION

Processions and parades were common events and popular spectacles in the past. There was no need to hold up streams of traffic for the Masonic Lodge or the Good Templars. Here the Templars are seen moving along Main Street at the beginning of the century, with the children's interest divided between the procession and the photographer. The first building on the right is the Burns Tavern, west of the Loudoun Arms. It later became the ice-cream parlour of George Ferri. Further along are the two buildings of the central premises of the Co-operative Society, now greatly altered.

THE FOUNTAIN

A drinking fountain for humans and horses was erected in 1890, as a gift to the town by Provost Joseph Hood, to mark the installation of a gravitation water supply from the reservoir at Loudoun Hill. It remained in position at Bridgend Corner until after the 2nd World War. Although the corner was one of the favourite stamping grounds for local men of leisure, the small piece of street theatre of the burgh workmen clearing a drain had induced them to move out from the Bridgend for a closer inspection. Another drinking well situated at the Cross, a gift of Miss Martha Brown of Lanfine, was removed in the late 1920's when a new entry to Todd the Plumber's workshops was driven through the building known as the Tontine House.

THE AULD TOONFUIT

Auld Newmilns lay virtually between the Toonheid and the Toonfuit seen here in 1893. The greatest change in this area occurred when the new Co-operative building with its imposing tower was opened in 1900, replacing the cottage and other buildings between the corner of High Street and Bridgend. On the left is Nisbet's Smiddy, later Beggs's Smiddy which continued in operation as a blacksmith's until after the Second World War.

FIRE AT THE STORE

In 1908, eight years after completion, the new Co-operative building at the corner of High Street and Main Street was destroyed by fire. It was immediately rebuilt and survives as an impressive feature among the traditional architecture of Main Street.

VIEW FROM THE NORTH

At the end of the last century looking from behind Loudoun Road towards the Lanfine side of the Valley, with the tileworks house still standing by Braehead Farm (Mount Pleasant). The factory chimneys from left to right are those of the old Clipping Mill (later the lace mill of Lawson & Goldie); Hood Morton & Co. and Haddow, Aird & Crerar, both of which were rebuilt after destruction by fire in the 1920's. The lade from Pate's Mill, seen running between these two factories to the Irvine, was the cause of a number of drowning fatalities among children in the neighbourhood.

OLD LOUDOUN MANSE

This is the rear view of the old manse on St. Margarets's Hill in 1895. A manse has occupied the site since the 17th century, but here the 18th century building dated 1768, is much as Robert Burns would have known it. The Rev. Dr. George Lawrie, the minister at that time was instrumental in keeping Burns in Scotland. When the poet visited the manse he slept in the room on the upper left of the building (seen in the photgraph with the window marked with a cross). He also composed a number of poems there, and scratched a compliment to Mrs. Lawrie on the window pane with the jewel of his ring. The window was damaged at an exhibition in 1949 during Civic Week.

THE SHOWS
The furthest west house at the end of last century was Gilfoot House shown here as Cadona's Shows are leaving the town after their annual visit. The horse drawn train of caravans was a show in itself and was a welcome event in the life of the town. On the left is a gate leading into a field where Gilfoot housing scheme now stands. On the right behind the row of trees was the field known as Mason's Holm, now also covered with council houses.

THE INDUSTRIAL REVOLUTION
After the introduction of machine lace to Darvel in 1875 and before the branch railway reached there, a number of lace firms built their factories on the flat land beside the river in Greenholm in the 1880's. In sequence viewed from the south-west are the Bleachworks of Forrest, Gillies & Co. (1883), Annabank Factory of R. Muir & Son (1882), Caledonia Factory of A. & J. Muir (1881), Vale Lace Works of Johnston Shields & Co. (1880), The Ayrshire Lace Co. of Stewart, Moir & Muir (1880), William Morton & Co. (1879) and Haddow, Aird & Crerar (1881). The print belongs to the early 1890's before the new school was built in High Street.

THE BLEACHFIELD

To meet the requirements of the growing lace and madras industry, Forrest, Gillies & Co. opened the Lanfine Bleaching and Finishing Works in 1883. The photograph shows the open nature of the site at Strath a dozen years later, looking across the railway at the works and some of the workers' houses. The view is north-west with Loudoun Manse among the trees the only house visible across the river. The water supply for the bleaching and finishing processes came from a private reservoir known as "The Vo" at Auchenruglen, now the only reminder of the business. Following an industrial dispute in 1932, the new owners, The Bleachers & Dyers Association, dismantled the works and moved their operations to Neilston. The buildings were used as a government store during the war and were destroyed by fire in 1945.

HERRIN NANCY'S

This is the cottage and orchard called Stanygate which lay on the left of the road on the way to Piersland Farm. It belonged to Herrin Nancy Scott who sold herring in a creel through the town, with the cry of "Herrin, fresh herrin". It fell into a ruinous state between the Wars and by the 1950's only the foundations and the neglected fruit trees remained.

THE STATION

Taken soon after the line opened to Darvel and before the station master's house and offices were erected, although the nameplates and advertising signs are in position on the new platforms. The passenger line terminated in the area which became the goods yard. The dark stone building seen over the roof of the goods depot was the mill of Stewart, Moir & Muir, destroyed by fire in 1915 and never rebuilt. The site became known as "The Burnt Mill," and is now part of the property of the Vesuvius Crucible Company.

THE AGE OF STEAM

A passenger train has just left the station in 1898. On the left is the River Irvine with only a single house to be seen at Strath. The first sheds of Goldie, Steel & Co. built the year before can be seen dimly beside the trees, but there is no Sam Gill, Cardcutters, or Morton, Young & Borland, Lace and Madras Manufacturers, whose mill was erected in 1901. The Bleachworks can be seen with its chimney, the tallest in the district, which inspired the puzzling question put to generations of children "How high is the Bleachworks lum?"

PATE'S MILL
"The lass o' Patie's Mill, Sae bonnie, blythe and gay."

One of the most noted buildings in Greenholm was Pate's Mill, demolished in 1977, and seen here in 1902. It was the first place to meet the eye of visitors or returning natives as they came down the Station Brae. The mill wheel, which was within the building, was driven by the lade which ran behind the houses on the south side of Brown Street. No commemorative plaque marks where the mill stood. It lives on only in Allan Ramsay's song.

BROWN STREET

When the handloom weaving trade prospered in the 19th century, restrictions on the Loudoun side of the river led to the expansion of Newmilns into Greenholm in Galston Parish. Fues were made available by the Browns of Lanfine and by 1870 houses had spread from Bridgend to the railway station. This view is from the west end, at the bridge over Pate's Mill lade.

THE RAILWAY HOTEL

All the trade for Newmilns and Darvel, between 1850 and 1896, not brought by carrier, came through Newmilns Station. The first refreshment place reached was the Lamlash Inn which became the Railway Hotel, seen on the right (now called the Riverside Inn). Beyond the opening to Nelson Street are two thatched cottages, now demolished. The one on the corner made way for the Post Office in 1908.

BEDLAM

This group of cottages still lies barely noticed, between the Tilework Brae and Brown's Road. Officially named Stewart's Place it was better known locally as "Bedlam". The photograph was taken in 1895 when the buildings looked very spruce and tidy. By the end of the 2nd World War they were greatly decayed and the last residents moved out soon after. They are now used as stores and workshops. In the background can faintly be seen the gas works chimney and the new school in High Street.

THE CRAIG

The railway was extended to Darvel in 1896. As can be seen here the viaduct over the Green had already been constructed, but three attempts were necessary to build a retaining wall of sufficient strength to hold the hillside at Mount Pleasant farm. When this was finally achieved by the host of masons and navvies seen here, the way was open for the first train on 1st June 1896. The wall is thirty-four feet high and thirty feet thick in places, and serves now with the viaduct only as relics of the engineering feats of the railway age. Between the arms of the crane in the foreground a number of local veterans can be seen, absorbed in the operation.

THE TOWN'S GREEN

Better known as the Big Green the last remaining portion of the old burgh of barony lands lies between the houses on the Greenside and the river. Being common ground burgesses could dry or bleach their laundry on it, but had to pay the old council for pasture. This photograph taken in 1893 gives a view of the area before the viaduct was built, causing the removal of the third house on the left at Greenhead. The factory chimneys are at Joseph Hood's in Main Street and J. & J. Wilson's at Greenhead. On the left at the end of the graveyard wall is the beaming shed of the Handloom Weavers' Association.

THE MILLER'S DAM
"Dae ye mind the miller's dam when the frosty winter cam?
We slid across the curlers' rink, and made their game a sham."

The dam for Pate's Mill was downstream from the Institute Brig a favourite spot for swimming in summer and curling in winter. The sluice outlet can still be seen at the corner of the Royal Bank gardens, but the dam itself was carried away in the flood of 1920. Although the author of the song "Lang, lang syne," the Rev. George Lawrie was recalling times at the beginning of the 19th century, the boys in the picture might also have been guilty of spoiling the curlers' game in winter in the 1890's.

INSTITUTE BRIG
Named for its proximity to Browns Institute, although it predates it by forty years, the bridge leads from Craigview Road to Browns Road and is the oldest surviving bridge in the town. In the foreground is one of the three bridges over the Norrel Burn, which runs across "The Green." By the steps is the old parish school and schoolhouse which closed as a school in 1874 and was replaced by the church halls in 1930. Beside it at the end of East Strand is the beadle's house, which is still standing.

THE BAUN HALL

At the east end of the graveyard in Greenside was the old beaming house of the Handloom Weavers' Association. In 1904 with handloom-weaving practically extinct the premises were gifted to the Town Council by the Co-operative Society and thereafter used as the Band Hall. Maggie Mair, the caretaker, also ran a shop in one of the front rooms. It was demolished in the 1960's, leaving the Band bereft of premises.

GREENSIDE

The runners in the foreground are competing in the annual Trades Races. The houses in the rear were all removed in the 1960's except the cottage on the far left. Three rights-of-way ran from the Main Street to the Green in this short distance. The two storey building on the right is Greenside House. Next to it is a thatched weaver's cottage built in 1800 and beyond it, with its numerous windows and large number of residents is the tenement known as "The Barracks."

THE TRADES' RACES

The races were begun in 1743 and were organised by elected office bearers of the Incorporated Trades of Newmilns. They were held annually on the Green until a few years after the railway viaduct cut it in half in 1895. After 1901 the races were arranged by the town council and moved to the Isles Public Park. It had been bought with the money paid in compensation by the railway company for the construction of the viaduct over the common land. The races, which had attracted professional runners and large numbers of spectators, did not survive the 1st World War and removal to a venue a half-mile from the town.

LADESIDE

The lade ran from the mill dam, past Loudoun Mill and the old 'Oo' Mill (Wool Mill), under the Green and back into the river. The path which ran beside it from Greenhead to the Mill Steps and on into Browns Road was a favourite Sunday afternoon walk. This view shows the Ladeside Cottages which still stand, but no longer in a rural backwater. The lade was a happy hunting ground for boys, guddling trout when the miller closed the sluice gates.

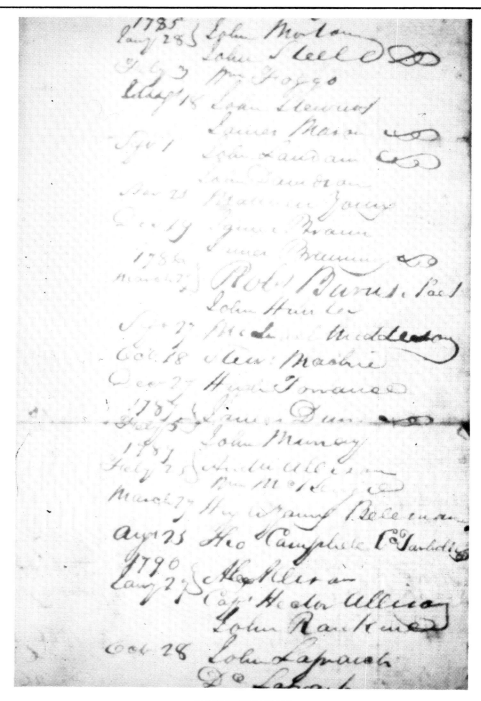

ROBERT BURNS

Robert Burns called in to Newmilns a number of times, befriended by the Rev. George Lawrie, who had advanced his career as a poet with introductions to the Edinburgh literati. On one of his visits Gavin Hamilton presented him to the local masonic lodge Loudoun Kilwinning No. 51 for honorary membership. The photograph reproduces the roll of new members around that period, showing the poet's name entered on 27th March 1786. Below the poet's name is that of John Hunter of Barrmill, Galston. He is reported to have met Burns at the masonic lodge and was known to him as the great-grandson of the hero of the ballad " I had a horse, I had nae mair."

```
1832   Alexander McLelland Teacher Kilmarnock
       William Wallace Agent Kilmarnock
Oct 26 J. G. Lockhart Teacher Troon
1829 Nov 3 William Cobbett Esquire, London (afterwards M.P. for Oldham)
Aug 12 J. Boswell Reid Weaver Newmilns
       James Allan         do
       William Richmond    do
       Andrew Borland      do
       James Auld          do
       John Adley          do
Oct 2  James Morton        do Son of Adam Morton
       Moses Smith Baker Son of Hugh Smith
       Nicol Brown Lawrie, Merchant Newmilns
1834   Robert Carrick Donaldson Surgeon do
Sept 26 Archibald Borland Labourer — do
       Mathew Main Weaver —           do
       Hugh Brown      do Son of John  do
       Charles Orr     do              do
       James Lyon —                    do
       William Brown   do              do
       Matthew Pollock do              do
       William Campbell do             do
       Alexander McPherson do          do
       John Borland —    do            do
       John Harris —                   do
       Alexander Gatey   do            do
27 —   William Miller                  do     do
Oct 4  John Lawrie                     do     do
       John Inglis                     do     do
       James Morton                    do     do
       John Borland                    do     do
       James Young                     do     do
       James Shaw                      do     do
       Thomas Young                    do     do
       John Campbell                   do     do
       James McGregor                  do     do
       Adam Meadows Flesher            do
       John Smith                      do
```

THE FREEDOM OF THE BURGH

The freedom of the Burgh was occasionally granted to famous men, admired by the burgesses. The name of David Dale, textile manufacturer and philanthropist, who had a family connection with Newmilns, is recorded in the Burgess Roll on August 12th 1792. But the person most respected, almost worshipped, by the townspeople in the period up to the passing of the Great Reform Bill of 1832 was William Cobbett, the radical leader. He was petitioned to visit the town in that year to address the people and was presented with the freedom of the burgh. His name has been inserted later giving the wrong date of 1829, among an assortment of paid-up members, mostly weavers, but also including two teachers, an agent, a merchant, a surgeon, a baker and a labourer.

LOUDOUN MILL

There was a corn mill on the site for four hundred years, in the hands of a Loudoun family from the earliest time, until the end of last century. The photograph taken in winter in the 1890s also shows the path leading down to the Mill Steps and, on the right, Townhead Farm, home of Wm. Smith who left the Smith Bequest for the poor of the Parish. There is no road into Pollock's factory which was not built until 1904. The mill ceased production in the 1960s with Mr J. Andrew the last miller. The wheel was removed in 1970, and the mill converted into dwelling houses.

DARVEL ROAD

One of the Darvel carriers is seen here on the new section of road in the 1890s. The old road lay further south and passed in front of Goosehorn Cottage. It was re-aligned when the railway was extended to Darvel, with new houses built on both sides. Further up, the road was widened in the 1920s at the place known as the Cut. At the foot of the hill on the left is Neil's Smiddy. The photograph was taken before the construction of Henderson, Morton & Inglis factory in 1898 and Burnford House in 1902. On the right are the houses at Townhead which have been twice replaced up to the present day.

ISLES STREET

Isles Street at the beginning of the century, looking east to Darvel. The narrowness of the road is apparent between the wooded embankments at Astinpapple. The corner of Campbell Street and Isles Street was a favoured meeting place for those who lived around the Townhead, and who were almost considered a separate community. The appearance and character of the area is greatly changed. All the houses on the left were replaced by council houses in the 1950s and 1960s, and new housing provided in West Campbell Street and Campbell Court. Behind the houses in Isles Street was The Beggaree, a model lodging house, where the last case of smallpox occurred. The victim was a travelling man for whom an isolation hospital was built at the Isles Public Park, and which served later as a changing room for the football teams. Only a few other cases were treated in this last outbreak of the disease in 1904.

MITCHELL'S CORNER

Mitchell's Corner in the 1900s between High Street and King Street where Tommy Mitchell had a shop, later occupied by Alex Currie. There were two other sweetie shops nearby to catch the trade of the children at the new school, the entrance to which was on the left. The houses between the school gates and Burn Road in High Street were demolished in the 1950s. The old properties in King Street between the corner shop and the Long Entry were equipped as a decontamination centre during the 2nd World War in the event of poison gas attacks. They disappeared completely after the War, and the area was landscaped.

THE SCHULE

A grand new school was built by Loudoun School Board in High Street in 1894, to replace Victoria School in Union Street. The architect was John Macintosh of Strath Mill who also took this photograph of the newly completed building. The bell and clock in the tower were added later. It looks here as many generations of pupils remember it, apart from the area in front, which was altered into three terraces with two sections of what was to become known as "the maister's grass," on which no small human foot dared to tread.

THE SCHOOL

The school that never was, from an early design of John Macintosh. It was probably never presented to the Loudoun School Board, being unsuitable for the projected location, unlike the long single-storey version which was accepted and built.

THE WATER WYND

The houses lying between Brown Street to the point where the road meets the river was named Nelson Street after the naval hero, and the part lying between Pate's Mill and the river was named North Devon Place. Between these and along the riverbank was Water Wynd. The cottages shown here at the corner, in a photograph from the 1900s, were replaced by council houses in the 1930s. The uncommonly low level of water in the river is explained by its loss to the lade which ran from the Miller's Dam at the Institute Bridge, behind Browns Street to Pate's Mill. Many of the old placenames were lost in the first quarter of the century, when in an early efficiency drive of the burgh council, a number of streetnames were combined in one.

THE BAND STAND

After the passing of the Towns Council (Scotland) Act at the beginning of the century and as a mark of civic pride it was decided to build a bandstand. It was placed on the river bank opposite the bowling green in Nelson Street. An ornate structure of ornamental ironwork and glass, it is seen here on opening day with the Band in attendance.

THE OLD SCHOOL STAFF

The old school staff, which moved to the new school from the old. Seated in the centre is Archibald Hood, headmaster, who had spent twenty years in Victoria School and was to spend another twenty in the new, before retiring in 1914.

In that year a pupil, John McMillan received a prize for six years perfect attendance. This, added to the total of the rest of his family, amounted to twenty-nine years without a single day's absence, in the time of all kinds of fevers and childish ailments.

DOITBURN STREET

It is difficult to believe that one hundred years ago many of the cottages in the town were still thatched. The thatch on those seen here in Doitburn Street in the 1890's appears to be in excellent condition but the houses now occupying the site at 11-13 High Street replaced the cottages at the beginning of the century. High Street now unites Doitburn Street which lay between Main Street and Drygate Street, Grey Street which ran from there to the corner of King Street, and the old High Street beyond that point.

A WHITE ELEPHANT

The choice of an exposed site, on the narrow strip of grass beside the river, doomed the bandstand from the beginning. It proved unpopular with the Band and the public alike, was used progressively less, and finally abandoned. Before the 1st World War, a group of youths reflected public opinion, by placing a model white elephant on its utmost pinnacle. After standing unused for years with roof, cupola and glass gone, the remaining ironwork was removed at the beginning of the 2nd World War.

T.T.

The temprance movement started up in the 1820s and campaigned against the use of alcoholic beverages, at a time when there were few licensing laws. The Temperance Hall was built in East Strand in 1859 with a branch attached of the Independent Order of Good Templars. Before the end of the century a local Band of Hope was holding meetings and concerts to influence children, and the British Women's Temperance Association was advocating total abstinence. This photograph from early in the 20th century is of the ladies of the local branch at their annual fete. In the left hand corner the cart belonging to Loudoun Springs, from the Newmilns Lemonade Works, is available to provide suitable refreshments.

LACE SHED

In 1872 there were 952 handloom weavers in the town, thirty years later there was barely a dozen. The introduction of lace, madras and other power-loom textiles saved the district from industrial decay. This is the interior of a lace shed at the beginning of the century with the dangerous overhead belt drive for the machines and the new breed of tenters, weavers, spoolers, brass winders, shuttlers and ravellers-aff who made up the personnel of the shed.

POWER-LOOM WEAVERS

While handloom weavers were almost exclusively men, when the power-loom version of the handloom was introduced to produce winceys, madras and tapestries the weavers were women. This group of workers of Hood, Morton & Co. pose with their loom tenter in the 1880s.

MADRAS WORKERS

Madras workers at J. & J. Wilsons's Greenhead Mills at the beginning of the century. The building on the left is the old "Oo" Mill, dating from the 18th century, water-powered from the lade for carding wool for Kilmarnock carpet makers. Later Wilsons tried to drive madras looms from the same source, but eventually installed a shaft from the steam engine in the main building to the right. The shaft ran under the road after the new mill was built in 1877 and may still be there today.

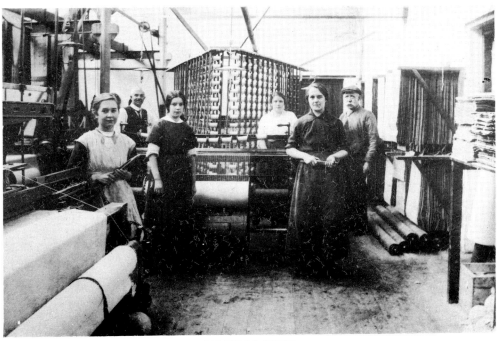

MADRAS SHED

Taken in Pollock's factory in 1918 the madras shed is typical of the period when many hundreds of women were employed in the production of madras, tapestries and similar goods. On the left is a young weaver at her loom. In the centre is a warping machine with its beam, and bank of bobbins. Hanging on the right are the cards for the Jacquard machines. Only one firm (Morton, Young & Borland) survives from a once thriving trade in madras.

LACE WORKERS

Although the personnel of the lace shed were men and boys, many of the oncost workers were women and girls. Apart from the male workers at the lace machines, women were required as spool and brass winders, and as drawers and darners in the grey rooms. Probably the whole day shift of William Morton & Co., Brown Street, is seen here in the 1920s.

WORKING CONDITIONS

The conditions in the lace mills were generally of a high order, in spite of the black lead used as a shuttle lubricant. The heavy rhythm of the lace machines was not unpleasant, and a communal spirit and many friendships were formed among the workers in each firm. The lace shed at William Morton & Co's factory shown here in the 1920s gives an impression of lace workers and their workplace. The young raveller-aff second from the right wears a jute bratty, to help pull out the loose threads in the shuttles.

DESIGNING ROOM

The lace mills were self-sufficient units from the moment the raw yarn was received until the cloth was despatched to the bleachers and dyers. One department involved in the conception of lace goods was the designing room where drafts of new patterns were drawn and copied. Here a designer and three copiers are shown in Henderson, Morton, Inglis factory at Darvel Road, in 1917. Nearest the camera, and ultimately chief designer, is W. Bennett Brown, choirmaster of the U.P. Kirk and a leading figure in the musical life of the town.

MASONS AND NAVVIES

The Glasgow and South Western Railway Co., employed some local men when the railway was extended from Newmilns to Darvel in the mid-1890s, but for the most part their railway builders were the famous navvies who travelled the country during the 19th century. These masons with apprentices and navvies were photographed at the building of the retaining wall at the Craig, and the bridge at the Tilework Brae in 1895.

THE SMIDDY

Three blacksmiths pose outside Neil's Smiddy, situated at the corner of Isles Street and Burn Road, (now the workshop and office of J. & T. McSkimming). Two or three blacksmiths' shops existed in each of the Valley towns to serve the large farming community, shoeing horses and repairing farm machinery. They also assisted in minor capacities, repairing gardening tools and making cleeks for children's girrs.

"ANYTHING FOR THE LAUNDRY?"

In the days of huge washings for large families most of the weekly task was performed by hand by the woman of the house. The customers of a laundry were likely to be the people who lived in the large houses, and a reason for a visit of the van of the Loudoun Laundry Company to the gatehouse of Lanfine. The laundry company had its premises in Clark's Pend off Main Street.

BONNY ROBERT AND HIS CUDDY

The rag-and-bone man was a well known figure in times when nothing was ever discarded without earning a few coppers. Newmilns had a famous practitioner in this trade at the turn of the century. Bonny Robert is seen here in Brown Street with his cart and scales, and his equally famous beast of burden, known only as his "cuddy," which was pastured in a small area of the Puddock Dub at the foot of Winnockland Brae.

THE WATTER CAIRT

The watter cairt was still required to tour the town after the introduction of piped water, when repairs were necessary and the pipes were regularly scoured, and was also used to lay the dust in the streets in dry summers. It was last seen during the 2nd World War at sports days on West End Park, providing cool drinks for thirsty competitors.

THE WATER TRIP
The great day for the provost, bailies and councillors, and the burgh officials was the water inspection carried out to oversee the proper maintenance of reservoirs and waterworks. In reality it was the annual shindig for the civic leaders, reward for their unpaid, hard-working efforts for the citizens throughout the year. The photograph taken at the turn of the century sees their departure in horse drawn brake, accompanied by kilted, top-hatted piper and outriders.

A BIG PARADE
The attractions of a parade were irresistable to the population. This one coming down High Street, perhaps to celebrate the relief of Mafeking or the coronation of Edward VII, is led by the Band and a burgh official with his halberd. Like most of the old pieces of civic regalia, this is now lost, or appropriated by the new council, thus reducing the pomp and ceremony and much of the pleasure of town life. On the right is the old hardware department of the Co-operative Society, at the head of the Store Wynd, built in 1881. Beyond it is the Parish Office where out-door relief of the poor was dispensed, and across from it, in part of Folley House, now demolished, was the local Pawn Shop.

BURGH OFFICIAL

The authority of the old burgh was proclaimed by the officers and constables employed by the council. They attended the councillors at courts and public events and proclamations, clothed in the emblems of office and carrying batons or halberds to keep the public in awe and small boys from mischief. There were two officers, two constables and a town crier who engaged attention with a drum. This was changed at a later date to a bell, and the bellman, as he came to be known, lasted into the era of the police burgh. Unlike the officer in the picture he had no badge of office. He was allowed to disappear from the town pageantry following the 2nd World War, after a claim for a wage increase of five shilling's for what was no more than an honorary appointment.

CO-OP BOOT SHOP

Shops selling footwear early this century were known more readily as boot, rather than shoe shops. Durability was an essential requirement when everyone walked everywhere for business or pleasure, apart from the occasional excursion by horse-drawn charabanc or train. It applied to women as well as men, and large stocks had to be carried, because fitting such an important item required care and deliberation. The ladies seen here were prepared to fit any number of boots or shoes, from vast resources on the premises, to satisfy a customer.

THE LAST HOUSE
The last house to the east was this cottage at Astinpapple on the road to Hillhead Farm. Like the cottages at Ladeside and Straith, Astinpapple was separate from the town. The house shown here was eventually surrounded by council and private housing and finally demolished.

THE WEST KIRK
The West Kirk was situated in High Street between the Co-op stables and the lane leading to Baltic House an area now occupied by the flats in High Street and West Church Street. There had been a Secession Church meeting house on the site since 1773. It was replaced by the Church shown here, built in 1833 and became known as the U.P. Kirk between 1847 and 1929. The congregation disbanded in 1961 and the Church with its attractive Georgian facade was pulled down soon afterwards.

LOUDOUN ROAD
Loudoun Road buildings remain much the same today as in the 1900s when this photograph was taken, but the character of the street as in other parts of the town is greatly changed by the disappearance of the hosts of children who lived and played in them. Families running into double figures are virtually gone, and the road which echoed to the sound of the occasional horse and cart is now in the sole possession of the motor car. The name too is changed. What is now part of Loudoun Road was Jeffrey Place on the left, and on the right, Jamieson Terrace.

FOOTBALL IN THE STREET
Every kind of sport and pastime was enjoyed on the road. There was insufficient space in the houses for large families to stay indoors. Life was lived in the streets, free from traffic danger, to play peevers and ba' beds, hunting and marbles, and the hundred other children's games now mostly forgotten. Football was frowned upon by the omnipresent town policemen, but sometimes, as in this photograph from the beginning of the century, a game would break out spontaneously. Here some fancy footwork is in evidence at the top of High Street right under Provost Pollock's civic lamp.

AULD FOLK'S TRIP
In the 1890s there were still no statutory holidays or retirement pensions. Old folk depended on private benevolence or charitable trusts for a little extra cash. Without these or family support it meant parish relief or the Puir's Hoose. An outing for the old ladies meant no more than a day in the country with tea provided at a farm or country house.

THE BURGH BAUN

The Burgh Baun seen here after winning 1st Prize at the Hamilton Contest in 1890. Established in 1833 it is the oldest brass band in Scotland still playing under the same flag. It suffered two breaks in continuity, at the eclipse of the handloom weaving trade in the 1880s, and following a depression in the lace industry in the 1960s. The photograph shows that by 1890 at its first re-birth it was again a successful outfit in smart uniforms and caps.

CYCLING CLUB

At the end of the 19th century a cycling craze spread throughout the country, especially after the invention of the safety bicycle with free wheel and pneumatic tyres. Men and women's fashion changed to meet the requirements of cycling as every young person dreamt of owning a bicycle, and knickerbockers, norfolk jackets and flat-heeled shoes came into vogue. Very soon the Pennyfarthing of the 1880s, seen here with members of the local club, were replaced by modern machines from Alex Todd's and Sanny Cochrane's, who specialised in one named "The Loudoun Rover".

THE MILL STEPS

Walking was the most popular form of recreation on summer evenings or Sunday afternoons. A favoured walk was on the Browns Road with access at the Institute Brig and the stepping stones at Loudoun Mill. Members of the Hood family of Rockpark are seen crossing on this print from the 1900s. The stones became redundant after the building of the Mill Steps Bridge in 1928.

SHARP SHOOTERS

Army reservists from the turn of the century, some of whom look like veterans of the Crimean War, have brought home the shooting trophy. This was another of the many sports and hobbies, practised by the population in a town rich in social activity and industry before the introduction of the cinema, radio and television.

THE WEST END

Loudoun Road is seen at the turn of the century when the town spread westwards and covered the flat land between Darnahill and the River Irvine. The houses were built mostly for the new managerial class, required for the fast developing machine-lace industry. On the right is the entrance to Willowbank Dairy, long in the possession of the Wallace family. The first two villas beyond it are in the characteristic style of architect, John Macintosh of Strath Mill. The railings which surrounded the front gardens of the houses were, as elsewhere in the town, carried off in the early 1940s as scrap-iron to make a contribution to the war effort.

TAM'S WELL

Around the town public wells were maintained at various points long after a piped-water supply had been introduced to every house and workplace. At the corner of the Green, by Persian Sands, was Tam's Well the choicest natural spring in the burgh. It was used for tea-making by the women living in the vicinity in preference over the water from the reservoir at Loudoun Hill. One old lady in Greenside continued to assert that there was "nae watter like the watter frae Tam's Well," even after she had been tricked with tea made from ordinary tap water. In this photograph, taken between the world wars, two women stand by the well, while children play in the river. The fence of the tennis court at Persian Sands can be seen through the trees on the right.

PLAYER EXTRAORDINARY

Hugh Wilson was a product of the old senior team and was capped straight from Newmilns against Wales in 1890. He moved on to become the inspiration of Sunderland in "The Team of all the Talents", but lost a number of caps, during the period in the 1890s, when professionals who moved to England were overlooked by their country. He returned to Third Lanark and played in their league winning side of 1903-04, and captained their team in the 1905 Cup final scoring twice in a 3-1 win over Rangers.

WEST END PARK

Local teams suffered from having their playing fields located some distance from the town, first at Hillhead then at Isles Public Park, and subsequently at the West End. This ground was opened by Major Shields of Glenrosa before the 1st World War with a game between the home team and Ardrossan. The pitch had one advantage. When Newmilns led in a cup-tie the ball had often to be retrieved from the nearby river. The pavilion disintegrated in the 1940s, and Masons Holm housing scheme was built on the field. No longer would we hear that popular call, "Pit the referee in the watter."

THE SENIORS

Before the Ayrshire Junior Football Association was formed in 1889 there were already senior teams in Newmilns, Galston and Hurlford. In 1902 the first Ayrshire Junior League had started with Newmilns and Darvel within its number. This photograph was probably taken in 1890 when Hugh Wilson was first capped for Scotland, and a few years before the senior team disbanded. By then the Scottish game had been greatly refined from ten years earlier, when in a letter to the editor of the local paper a reader complained that "now the winter season is coming on we shall hear of fresh serious and fatal accidents in that brutal game called football. In my opinion 'charging', 'tackling' and 'carrying' the ball in the hands should be done away with by mutual arrangement of all the principal clubs."

ESCOCES FOOTBALL CLUB

The firm of Johnston, Shields & Co., not only carried the art of lacemaking to Spain when it established a factory in Barcelona in 1893, it also took with it the football skills of its workers. Very quickly the Spaniards learned enough of the game for the usual league competitions to be arranged, but in season 1900-01 the Escoces Football Team still maintained superiority to win the Spanish Cup the first time it was run. In the team photograph taken at Baranova near Barcelona, are five young men from Newmilns, including George Girvan (front row, centre) later Provost of the town and Secretary of the Lace Union, flanked by the brothers Alex and John Black. Johnston, Shields also had a factory in Gothenburg, Sweden and in 1891 most of the members of the newly created Gothenburg F.C. were from Newmilns.

TEENAGERS' PICNIC

Picnics during the summer months were important features of the social scene at the end of the 19th and well into the 20th century. Here a light hearted group of young men and women are snapped by the side of the Burnawn with a basket of provisions and a football. In the middle row third from the right is Richard Jamieson, in later years Provost of the town. Other favourite sites for picnics were Croden Glen, the Hogging Craig, round by Robin's and further afield at the Cairn.

VOLUNTEERS

No record has been kept of the survivors of this group photographed at the beginning of the 1st World War. The volunteers and reservists were the first to be mobilised. They were called up before the introduction of conscription in 1916 and many were lost or wounded in France or the Dardanelles. Others pressed into service were killed in the battles in Flanders in 1917-18. In the centre, front row, is Captain Morton of Winnockland, and of the firm of William Morton & Co., lace manufacturers.

LAND GIRL

During the 1st World War many jobs in factories and on the land, normally held by men, were undertaken by women in a strange process called "dilution of labour". While men were in France and Flanders, a Women's Land Army was created for work in the countryside. One of its members is seen here, at the cemetery gates, returning to a farm after her milk round.

THE WAR MEMORIAL

After the 1st World War monuments were raised in every town and village in memory of the large numbers killed in the conflict. The terrible impact of that War on a small community can be understood from the loss of 138 young men between 1914-18, compared with the 40 names added for those who died between 1939-45. The town memorial was placed in the front of Lady Flora's School soon after the 1914-18 war and unvieled in a ceremony still recalled each year in the Armistice Day parade and service. After the 2nd World War the surrounding area was enhanced by a memorial garden.

RECREATION GROUND

The Bleachwork Company provided a bowling green and tennis court, as an early example of an employees' welfare scheme, at the riverside opposite Glenrosa. This attractively laid-out area quickly became derelict, and the clubs were disbanded, after the company closed its works in 1932. The pavilion still stands and has been used as an Electricity Board store and a lace company's millshop. Other tennis courts were available in the 1930s at Lady Flora's Institute and the Persian Sands.

LADIES' DAY

Ladies' Day at the Bowling Club in the 1920s when women participated only in the more decorous forms of sport. The club was established in 1862 and continues to thrive, while other games such as curling and quoits declined. The gap in the houses at the end of Wilson Place led to the garage of John Mair, Carrier. On the left on the horizon at Borebraehead is the U.P. Kirk manse, while in the foreground, neglected, but still intact, is the Band Stand.

THE MILL TRIP

The Mill Trip was an outstanding event in the year, when each factory had a day out, usually at an Ayrshire coastal resort. A factory outing, the Store gala day, and the Sunday-school trip allowed a welcome change of scene for those who could not afford a full week on holiday at the Fair for the whole family. The photograph shows the grey-room workers of J. & J. Wilson's in the 1930s "in for a paidle" accompanied by their department manager.

HUNGRY THIRTIES

With mass unemployment and the introduction of the Means Test the early 1930s were difficult for men out of work and their families. A branch of the National Unemployed Workers' Movement was formed in the town and a local contingent regularly joined the hunger marches. Members are seen getting ready to regroup outside the Co-operative Society's halls to march to a demonstration, undeterred by the winter conditions.

THE NEW POLITICS

Following the radical tradition of the 19th century delegates from Newmilns attended the early conferences of the original Scottish Labour Party formed in 1888 and of the Independent Labour Party in 1893. Early campaigners who came to the town were Keir Hardie, Cunninghame Graham, John MacLean and James Maxton. The Newmilns and District Textile Workers' Union, along with the local branch of the I.L.P., supported visits of the Forward Socialist Van seen here after the 1st World War with it's stock of literature and volunteers promoting the sale of the Scottish independent socialist newspaper "Forward". Meeting's were also arranged with a distinguished speaker for the evening of the visit.

THE JAZZ AGE

Between the wars a new fever spread from America and infected the dancing public. Bands sprang up everywhere, copying the styles of the great jazz musicians, readily available on gramophone records. In the twenties every family had to own a gramophone and in the thirties, a wireless. The bands were recruited from the host of local pianists, violinists and brass bandsmen, who quickly mastered the music and the new voice of the saxaphone. With the addition of a drum kit, dancers could soon shimmy to the fox-trot and the quick step. A local group was known as the Loudoun Crodaens posing here before a charity dance in Loudoun Castle in the early thirties. From left to right: W. Leitch, piano; R. Paton, violin R. Paton senr., clarinet; John Comrie, trombone; T. Robertson, violin; J. Rigby, trumpet and P. Murray, drums.

THE JUNIORS

"Come awa', come awa',
The boys in green an yella,
The day we beat the Buffs..."

One of the casualties of the depression was the local junior football team. The part-remembered rhyme above, speaks of the team colours and commemorates the great days when Newmilns won the Ayrshire Cup four times in the first decade of this century, beating Kilwinning Rangers, the Scottish Cup holders, in season 1909-10. The photograph shows the last Newmilns Junior Team, taken at Galston, before it finally wound up in season 1930-31.

THE 1920 FLOOD

August 1920 was the last occasion on which the River Irvine flooded the lower parts of the town, entering houses, halls and factories, and damaging roads and bridges. In this scene the floodwaters pass along Greenside. In the centre is the Hebron Hall, meeting house of the local Christian Union, and later the British Legion Club until destroyed by fire in 1972. On the right is the Masonic Lodge, Loudoun Kilwinning No. 51, which dates back to 1747. In a minute of a meeting for 27th March, 1786 is the entry, "Much to the satisfaction of the Lodge, Mr Robert Burns, Mossgiel, Mauchline, introduced by the Right Worshipfull, was admitted as a member". The master at the time was Gavin Hamilton the poet's friend.

KILNHOLM STREET

Kilnholm Street showing the damage caused by the flood in August 1920. The river has bitten its way halfway across the street, taking with it the wall which was replaced by railings. At the same time it carried away an arch of Brown Street bridge, and the Miller's Dam. Beyond the cottages on the right is Wilson Place, and the three-storey Glesca Buildings, named for their resemblance to city tenements unusually high for a country town. Built on a shelf by the river, by their sheer weight they have proved unstable, and were partly demolished in 1986.

MILL FIRE

Over the years lace factories proved very combustible. This fire in 1923 affected Haddow, Aird and Crerar's and William Morton's in Brown Street. It attracted the usual large number of onlookers, to view from the vantage point of the railway goods yard. On the left is the coal-ree bothy and on the right, saved from the flames, Pate's Mill.

THE RAILWAY

The Station, which had opened in 1850, saw fewer customers with the improvement in bus services from the 1930s, but heavy goods, coal, mail and parcels continued as a lucrative source of income. The photograph, looking east, shows the goods yard, sheds, offices and coal depot to the left. A passenger train is leaving the station with its waiting rooms, ticket office, signal box, station house and footbridge. This whole area is now covered by the building of the Vesuvius Crucible Company.

THE IRON BRIG

The first footbridge over the Irvine was erected in 1881 between Loudoun Road and Nelson Street to give mill workers easier access to the Greenholm factories and was called the Iron Brig in contrast to the two older stone bridges upstream. On the left are Brown's Buildings demolished in the 1960s, along with the two-storey buildings on the other side of the river. The bridge seen here in the 1920s was replaced after the 1954 flood made it unsafe.

THE SURGERY

Dr. Aird's surgery in the 1920s with its ornate lamp above the door and its dispensary on the premises. Those were the days when the roads and pavements were in good shape, and a doctors' consultation fee was 1/–. The untrained staff made up the prescriptions with no recorded fatalities. Dr. Simpson followed in the practice from the end of that decade, for the next forty years, and the surgery moved to the old parish office in High Street.

THE BOTTOM STORE

By 1900 the Co-operative Society had opened branches at the top and bottom of the town. The bottom store in Jamieson Terrace (now 30 Loudoun Road) is shown here in 1912 with its staff of four, and a butchers' roundsman. It is still stands under new owners. There was another grocery branch at the end of King Street and latterly at Gilfoot.

THE JOINERS

The three main joinery firms in the town were Mitchell, Black and Wallace & Torrance. The last named had premises at 28-30 Brown Street, shown here in the 1920s. The pend led to the works at the rear, while the shop on the left specialised for a while in gramophones and records. Standing in the centre is Mr. W. Torrance the proprietor and on the right is Willie "Pal" Torrance, a well known character about the town and driver of "The Wee Rid Barra", of the local fire brigade.

MAGGIE AULD'S

The interior of the shop at 110 Main Street, east of Loudoun Church, was a centre of attraction. Children could buy from the glass jars, wine gums, all-sorts, mints and chocolate drops, along with other favourites, toffee balls, teuch-jean and liquorice. Behind the jars are the comics and weekly papers the Adventure, Topical Times, People's Friend and My Weekly, while on the wall rack are the magazines known as Penny Dreadfuls or Tuppenny Horribles. By the 1930s these cost 4d or 6d. The shop and neighbouring houses were knocked down in the 1960s.

COCHRANE'S CORNER

The shop at No. 1 High Street of A. Cochrane & Son which sold hardware over three generations. At the rear were the warehouse and upholstery workshop. At its height the business employed more than any other retail outlet apart from the Co-operative. Mr Alex Cochrane the founder is seen here with his son William.

CO-OP CENTRAL PREMISES

The first Co-operative society in the town started in 1840, but did not survive long. The present society was established in 1856 and by 1866 built the central premises in Main Street. By 1881 it had extended along the Store Wynd to the hardware department in High Street, and had taken in an adjoining building in Main Street. In this 1920s photograph the staff of the grocer's shop pose for posterity.

THE BUTCHER'S VAN

A number of the Co-operative Society's departments had outside salesmen, requiring a way with horses. Coal, baking, butcher meat, fruit and vegetables and fish were delivered by horse van round the town and countryside. In this print the butcher's van is at rest on Darvel Road, taken in the late 1920s. During the winter the horses were kept in stables at the corner of High Street and Drygate Street, and in summer grazed in the park beside the school, now used as a ski-slope.

BICYCLE REPAIRS

M. Todd and A. Cochrane were the two main retailers of bicycles. Such were their popularity for work and play that Todd's were able to employ a full-time repair man, before and after the 1st World War, at the premises on Main Street. They also supplied petrol for the occasional motor vehicle, and on one day in 1914 came to the rescue of an aviator when his plane ran out of fuel and made a forced landing in a field on Browns Road.

OLD VICTORIA SCHOOL HOUSE

The last remaining part of the old Victoria School built in 1874 was the schoolhouse in Burn Road. The school which lay behind it was in the line of the railway and was removed in 1895. The schoolhouse remained as a dwelling house until the 2nd World War when it was designated the official mortuary, and billets for troops in transit. It was cleared away after the war.

THE LAST THATCH

The last thatch is being removed from the roof of the cottages at 11 and 12 Kilnholm Street in the early 1930s. Considered a hazard to health and safety, owners were urged by the council to replace straw with slates, and the old theekers (thatchers) became a dying breed in this part of the country.

THE NEW PIT
Although there were two ingaunees (drift mines) over the river near Windyhill Farm, the New Pit on the Woodhead road was the only pit near the town. Most of the men in this picture taken at the pithead buildings in the 1920s were from Galston with its pool of skilled mineworkers. The flooding of the pit led to the abandonment of the Galston pits on the Loudoun side of the river. Coal was conveyed from it by the "Bogey Line", on an endless chain, to the railway at Newmilns.

THE OLD MEN'S CABIN
The old men's cabin was opened in 1930 built from funds raised by public subscription. Its size did not take into account Scotland's ageing population, nor did anyone forsee that the separation of the sexes in social life might become unfashionable. Situated beside the river in Browns Road it required a large extension in 1985.

THE YOUNG BOYS' POOL
The Staners was the favourite swimming pool for the boys of the town, half-way to Darvel on the Browns Road. Apart from its sunny position, it had the added attraction of being the first deep part of the river above the outlet from the sewage works on the site of Greensmill.

COVENANTERS' MONUMENT
The Covenanters' Monument was unveiled on 26th April, 1913 commemorating the 10 men of Loudoun Parish killed by the government between the years 1666 and 1685 for their attachment to their religious faith. The monument is in Loudoun Parish kirkyard in Main Street.

A PECULIAR HOUSE

A peculiar house stood in High Street at the head of Burn Road. Some of the stonework in its construction was recovered during the demolition of the old parish church in 1844. The pillars on each side of the front door formed a unique feature for a cottage. They had been part of the entrance to the parish church and were regarded as a curiosity until the house was demolished in the early 1950s. On the left down Burn Road was Young's Dairy and like Notman's in King Street, Auld's in Isles Street and Browning's in Riverbank Street one of the many small dairies within the town boundary. These were later replaced by farmers with milk rounds. Duncan of Hillhead, Wallace of Cronan, Lindsay of Brownhill, Weir of East Heads, Brown of Windyhill and Muir of Molemount.

BY THE GREEN

Two of the oldest houses in the town are seen here after the 2nd World War and before they were replaced by council houses in the 1960s. On the right is Greenside House and in the centre a cottage built in 1800. Behind the double doors a passage led to the premises of Joseph Hood, Engineers. There was also at the rear of the cottage a room housing the last handloom in the town which had lain unused for thirty or forty years. On the left is the tenement known as the Barracks, behind which in a workshop belonging to Kerr Brothers, Painters, a dozen women were employed in the 1920s, colour stencilling the pattern on lace curtains and tablecloths.

OLD AND NEW

Astinpapple, now generally spelt Alstonpapple, with Hillhead, was a village separate from the town until new houses were built in Darvel Road. The cottages on the right still survive, although modernised, while on the left are the council houses known as Isles Terrace. With Isles Street the name is derived from the Isles farm which was situated between the Burflat and Norrel burns and was owned by the family of Stewart in the late 18th Century. The earliest council houses were built in the late 20s and early 30s at Kings and Queens Crescents, Isles Terrace and Campbell Street under the supervision of Burgh Surveyor, James Gilmour. It proved the end of an era as brick and harling replaced stone as the major building material.

CHURCH INTERIOR

After the 2nd World War many congregations decided to improve the plain appearance of their churches. Light and finely carved woodwork and furniture were introduced, with communion tables, lecterns and fonts, with rich drapery and stained glass added. This print from that time shows some of the innovations at Loudoun East Church with the Morton commemorative window on the right. Apart from religious observance the town's churches had numerous social functions. Their organisations normally included a Men's Club, Women's Guild, Youth Fellowship, Sunday School, either Scout and Guide troops or Boys Brigade and Life Boys. They held Christmas and choir concerts and nativity plays and an annual Sunday School Trip. There were also the Christian Union, Plymouth Brethren and Salvation Army, all contributing to the Christian influence on the life of the community.

THE LACE STRIKE

The Lace Strike which lasted for five months in Newmilns in 1897, created discord in the community, the introduction of strike-breakers, and an exchange of scurrilous pamphlets and posters between the employers and the union. The best known of these, issued by the lace manufacturers, is reproduced here. In the top right-hand corner it shows Graeme Hunter, leader of the imported strike-breakers, with the union officials and sympathisers lampooned under their respective nick-names.

CAUTION

It is the interest and duty of every Person in the Factory to prevent WASTE OF MATERIALS, particularly WEFT, and any neglect in this respect will be visited with INSTANT DISMISSAL besides paying for the articles destroyed.

GOOD OLD DAYS

Although the new lace industry brought full-employment to the district at the end of last century, a stern discipline was maintained over the workers in the lace and madras mills. In the earliest days there was a six-day working week, from Monday morning up till Saturday evening, with an average lace weaver's wage of £1 per week. The tradition of fines by agents over the male weavers in the hand-loom days continued with the employers of female madras operatives on the power loom. They were warned not to waste the more expensive weft yarn under threat of instant dismissal. This copy from a page of a piece-work book tells all.

FREE KIRK

Free Kirk or Loudoun East Church in King Street was held in great affection by its congregation. It was built in 1846 three years after the disruption in the Church of Scotland when large numbers could no longer remain in the established church. Traditionally envangelical, its ministers often brought great sporting personalities, such as Eric Liddell and Tommy Walker, to inspire the youth of the town. When the congregation was re-united with Loudoun Parish Church in 1980, the building was not retained and was demolished in 1983. The photograph shows it with its avenue of trees in the years between the wars.

THE TAILOR'S

Up until a few years after the 2nd World War townspeople could obtain most of their needs locally. They could also have their clothes made at Willie Deans's tailor shop at the corner of Browns Street and Browns Road. Seen here in the centre, with members of his staff, he was a man of many parts and the last of the town's great characters. The photograph is taken in the garden behind the corrugated iron workshop, part of which formed the premises of J. Brown, slater and builder. In the background is Stewarts Place, (Bedlam).

THE WILDERNESS
The old buildings on the left along with the other houses further up Kilnholm Street were on the area known as "The Wilderness". They were replaced by council flats in the 1960s. On the right is Richmond's Corner named after the brothers, Richmond who kept the shop after retiring from the music halls as musicians and entertainers, billed as Barton and Franklin. In the centre in Hillside Place is the gas works. The chimney and gas holder were prominent landmarkers at the time of this photograph in the 1940s, before their removal with the arrival of natural gas. The quiet housing scheme now occupying the site is Covenanters Court.

THE CINE
The Cine or the old picture house and also known as the talkies, or the flicks was built in 1913 and continued to operate until a few years after the 2nd World War. The first performance had in its attractive programme: "The Stolen Treaty" - A Great Drama, "Paul Sleuth" - Thrilling Detective Drama. The aim of the proprietor was "to interest, elevate and amuse". Prices were Front Area 2d., Middle Area 4d., Back Area 6d., Children half price. The facade has since been removed, along with the buildings between the picture house and King Street corner, which is now the forecourt of the Townhead Garage. Beyond it encroaching on the Main Street is the house and fish and chip shop of Luigi Valentini, while on the right is the first house in Isles Street with the shop of J. Black, Joiner.

PROJECTIONIST

Projectionist was a new word coined for a unique post among the servants of the silver screen. This pre-war photograph is of the rear exit of the old picture house and the balcony outside the projection room. Sam Hill, for many years manager of the old and new picture houses, is on the left holding a reel of film. The exit led on to a passage which emerged on King Street, and an area once waterlogged and known as the Puddock Dub. The highlight of the week for children was the Saturday matinee with its exciting serials of Flash Gordon or the adventures of Rin-Tin-Tin, preceding a main feature of a cowboy favourite such as Ken Maynard or Buck Jones. In the early years of the 2nd World War the matinee still cost only two pence (old money), compensating a little for the disappearance of sweets and chocolate from the shelves of the town's shops.

GILFOOT

Gilfoot was built in the years 1936 to 1939 and with its 172 houses solved the problem of overcrowding. For some time afterwards many of the streets of the town were unnaturally quiet as large families moved to new homes at the west end. After 1945 the problem returned with what was described as the post-war bulge in population. To accommodate the numerous young families another council scheme was built on the southern side of the main road at Masons Holm. Gilfoot was a source of pride to the burgh council in its general layout, semi-rural setting and background of "Loudouns bonnie woods and braes".

POLIS STATION

The outpost of the Ayrshire Constabulary was in King Street and is now converted into two private houses. Built early in the century it has the arms of the County of Ayr within the door pediment and a stone plaque above. The upper flat was a sergeant's house, with the office on the ground floor. A sergeant and three constables were the station complement for both Newmilns and Darvel, but normally only one constable on duty was enough to keep boys and youths in a town in fear and trepidation, ensuring the development of worthy and respectable citizens. The photograph was taken during or just after the 2nd World War as the small louvered box on the cell roof to the right housed the air-raid siren. For a while after the war it was the alarm to call out the fire-brigade.

AIR RAID SHELTER

On some vacant sites in the town air-raid shelters were built to safeguard the population from enemy bombing raids during the 2nd World War. One of these can be seen behind the baffle wall on the right in High Street. It was claimed that occupants would survive all but a direct hit, but it is doubtful if anyone ever used it during a raid, or the others situated at East Strand, Townhead the Wilderness and Gilfoot. The door with the advertisement beside it on the opposite side of the street is the entrance to Jim Elliot's sweet shop, demolished in the mid 50s with the neighbouring houses.

A BOMB CRATER

The town could not have been described as an important centre of war production, although innumerable mosquito nets were produced in the lace mills and tank wheels made in Hood's engineering shop. There were also government stores at the Bleachfield and other factory building's. Soldiers were billeted in the town and trained in the vicinity up until the invasion of Europe. The local headmaster reported that eighteen bombs fell in Loudoun parish early in the war, but these fell harmlessly mostly on Loudoun Moor. One huge bomb which did alarm the population and blew out shop windows in the town fell in a field south of Hodge's farm, Loudoun Mains and left the crater seen in the photograph.

LOCAL HERO

It is difficult to comprehend that forty young persons from the town were killed during the years of the 2nd World War. Casualties were high among men who volunteered for the R.A.F., and who were soon in air-crews. Other servicemen were wounded and some taken prisoner by the Germans and Japanese. The photograph catches a happier moment in the military career of Sergeant Thomas Turner of Greenside as he is decorated for bravery in the field soon after the invasion of France. He is being presented with the Military Medal by Field-Marshall Bernard Montgomery.

THE MODERN TOWN

Although the three burghs of the Irvine Valley were largely industrial, they had been compared with small market towns with their mixture of old and new buildings and tidy appearance. Even in the 1930s in a time of depression the Main Street has an air of well-being and activity. In almost every building eastwards some form of enterprise was in operation. On the left side alone from Adam Wyllie, grocer; there was Semple, fruiterer; through the entry and upstairs was Mr. Oliver, dentist; next was the shoe shop of the Misses Mitchell; followed by John Loudoun, baker; beyond the wooden hoarding was Hugh Cruden, cobbler; and through the pend, Alex Campbell, carrier; and then Betty's sweet shop in part of the Commercial Hotel.

THE AMERICAN FLAG

The American Flag being presented during the Civic Week celebrations in 1949 replaced the original given by Abraham Lincoln to the Newmilns handloom weavers in 1864. Although their livelihood depended on the import of raw cotton from the southern states, and was virtually unobtainable during the American Civil War, the weavers formed an Anti-Slavery Society and sent a petition of support to Lincoln. In return they were presented with a flag and two testimonial volumes from the President of the United States. In the picture R. M. Paterson, on the right, chairman of the Civic Week Committee, and headmaster of Newmilns School, displays the new flag given to replace the old by Mr. D. C. McDonough, the U.S. Consul General.

CIVIC WEEK

After the last war but still in the dark days of rationing and all kinds of shortages a committee was formed in 1949 to organise a full week of festivities to brighten the townsfolks lives and bring exiles home for the first time for many years. It was probably the last time the town will see such a great communal effort, for the large majority of organisation in existence then have dwindled away. Part of the programme was a procession of groups in period costume and floats with tableaux depicting the history of the town. It took months to prepare, and presented 24 separate items. The procession is seen passing the Loudoun Arms with the group representing the ten Convenanting Martyrs of Loudoun Parish, followed by the float which carried the "Lass o' Patie's Mill."

FLOOD IN UNION STREET

In 1954 the town's coup at Isles Public Park slipped into the Norrell Burn and was carried into Darvel Road, Main Street, Union Street and Burn Road. It brought with it uprooted trees, dead animals and twenty years accumulation of rubbish. The view is of Union Street a few days later when the choked conduit under Burn Road caused a second flood of rain water, and helped to carry much of the noxious debris into the River Irvine.

THE PREFABS

Prefabricated houses were erected after the 2nd World War to help reduce the housing shortage. Those shown here are at Persian Sands at the time of the 1954 flood, while the Big Green was still covered with rubbish carried down from the coup. The old woolen mill in the centre and the prefabs were cleared away for new housing as were the other prefab sites at Mill and Strath Crescents.

BIRD'S EYE VIEW

Bird's eye view of the Townhead taken at the time of the 1954 flood. It shows Campbell Street and Union Street under layers of mud. Prefabs are seen still standing in Mill Crescent, and there are no new houses in Ladeside. A number of old houses can still be seen in Campbell Street and Isles Street, but council housing would soon alter this area of the town.

STRANDED
The force of the flood of rubbish and dirt from the coup can be seen in this picture of a bus brushed aside into a hedge in Darvel Road with mud splattered up to the top deck. In the boiler room of Henderson, Morton, Inglis' factory on the left the suddenness of the inflow almost trapped and drowned a worker. The wall of mud carried trees and other heavy objects down Main Street as far as East Strand, surprising the citizens, who thought the river Irvine had been tamed since the 1920s' unaware of any danger from the Norrel Burn.

CAMPBELL STREET CORNER
This print shows the size of the flood-borne objects in 1954 at the corner of Campbell Street and Isles Street. Behind the house on the left is an outside stair; once a common feature of the town architecture. All the tenements at the lower end of the street have now been replaced by council houses but early in the century they had formed a close-knit little community of its own. From one entry further up the street there used to emerge every morning for school, thirty three children. Today, seventy years later, there can be little more than that number in the whole street.

THE FIRST DAY

Children hurry home after the opening of the new school in 1894. Held in affection by generations of scholars, it stood for almost seventy years and symbolised a great movement forward in Scottish education with the development of town schools. Up to the end of its existence many who left to find work in the local lace mills and workshops had been introduced to the pleasures and complexities of the French language, and had learned something of Caesar's wars in the original tongue.

THE LAST MORNING

Fire destroyed the school in High Street in 1960 and struck a blow at civic pride. The large proportion of timber in the building produced a spectacular blaze in the high wind and reduced it to a shell by morning, when children arrived for class. After a temporary stay in local halls, the primary classes moved to the new edifice at the West End, while the secondary pupils went further west to Loudoun Academy.

THE DOWN TRAIN

The down train from Darvel normally pulled in on the other track, a familiar sight to the thousands over the years going off to work, on holiday, or to the football games. By 1963, the mail bags and railway workers were the main customers in the passenger trains. Up the line is the Tilework Brig and on the right among the trees is Mount Pleasant Farm.

THE RAIL BUS

The pleasures of rail travel were nearly at an end for Valley folk, when the small diesel rail bus was introduced in the early 1960s. The aim was to cut costs and keep custom on the branch line to Kilmarnock, but passengers preferred the buses and the Beeching cuts carried everything away. On the left in the picture is Laigh Dalloy with Windyhill Farm behind it. Below the farm is the waste bing of the old inguanee mine, another relic of the Valley's industrial past.

THE REX CINEMA

The Rex Cinema opened in the first week of the 2nd World War, in September 1939, with the film "Alexander's Ragtime Band". It immediately shut down again on a government order that all places of entertainment close because of the danger from bombs to large numbers of the public in confined places. This was quickly repealed as maintaining good morale during wartime was seen as a higher priority. Along with the old picture house further up the street, it was soon showing to packed audiences. Both picture houses belonged to the Young family and the Rex, built on the site of the old Cross Keys Inn, was the last word in spectator comfort. A greater danger to the cinema was the spread of T.V. reception throughout the country. The Rex held on tenaciously, and for a while alternated between bingo and film shows, but what had been the most attractive little film theatre in the Valley finally succumbed, and the last films were shown in 1986.

CHARACTER IN STONE

The individual character of a town depends upon the continued existence of its unique buildings, maintained in good condition for its original purpose or an alternative use. Lady Flora's Institute in Main Street was built in 1875 as a school for the girls of the town, in memory of Lady Flora Hastings of Loudoun Castle, a victim of slander at the court of Queen Victoria. In 1921 it was converted into an institute for educational and recreational activities and remained an asset to the eye and the needs of the community until closed in 1981. The burgh council accepted the newly laid out gardens in front of the Institute in 1951, from the Civic Week Committee, as part of their continual endeavour to improve the appearance and amenity of the town.

MILL COTTAGE

Mill Cottage in the centre of this recent photograph was once isolated from the town while the mill itself has been converted into flats. The legend "No mill, no meal" on the wall is no longer valid as, with the advent of the super-store and cheap travel, few products are now made in the district for home consumption. The mill lade has been filled in and houses built on it. The meal mills ceased production in the 1960s with the retirement of Archie Smith and John Andrews, the last representatives of the millers who had given the town its name.

HILLHEAD ROAD

With the completion of Masons Holm no more large housing schemes were required, and instead the council provided homes in small level areas within the burgh at Strath, Mill Crescent and Ladeside. Private builders had to find sites wherever they could, at the top of Borebrae or, as in this photograph of the 1980s, on the side of hills. The view south over Lanfine Woods compensates for the difficulty of access. A willingness to overcome construction problems was proof that many believed the town was still a pleasant place to settle and live.

A FINAL VIEW

A final view of the Burgh of Newmilns and Greenholm, taken from the air in the 1960s. The railway track has been removed and temporary school buildings still occupy the old playground in High Street. Other changes can be seen in the area of this photograph, covering the street plan of the town laid down over the centuries, while the earlier prints in the book have shown the life and work of the people and the appearance of the streets and buildings. This is the stage reached after almost five hundred years as an independent burgh. Only time will judge how well Auld Newmilns compared with the new.